THE FAMILY &
THE STATE

A critical introduction for Childhood Studies

Rob Creasy

Independent

Copyright © 2020 Rob Creasy

All rights reserved

No part of this book may be reproduced, or stored in a retrieval system, or transmitted in any form or by any means, electronic, mechanical, photocopying, recording, or otherwise, without express written permission of the publisher.

ISBN: 9798650861300

CONTENTS

Title Page	1
Copyright	2
Chapter 1 The Family	5
Chapter 2 Parenting & Failing Families	26
Chapter 3 Escaping poverty: Social Mobility & Life-chances	54
References	91

Acknowledgements

Many thanks to Fiona Corby of Teesside University, Emma Walker of York St John University and Yasmin Stefanov-King of Coventry University, Scarborough for advice and guidance.

How it ended up in this format owes much to the erudite discussions held over lunch at York St John University and the wise words of Julian Stern, Tony Leach & Jeff Buckles. Jeff was nearly right.

CHAPTER 1 THE FAMILY

1.1   The Family

This book is one of a series that is aimed at students studying childhood with UK Higher Education, whether that be on a course such as a BA Childhood Studies or on some other course reflecting work within the wider children's workforce such as a Foundation Degree in Working with Children and Young People, or Early Years. The aim of the book is to introduce and explain some key issues and concepts alongside offering a critical introduction to the relationship between children, families and the state. It also aims to provide some guidance to students on how to use what you have read in academic assignments.

For anyone studying childhood or children in general it seems perfectly reasonable to also consider families but a consideration of the state may not always seem so obvious. I trust that I will be able to explain why it is as the book progresses. Trust me, it is very relevant.

In considering the relationship between the family and the state we really ought to be able to define what these are. I will define the state much more fully in Creasy (2020a) Family, State and Policy but a basic definition is that a state exists when there is a political system in place governing over a definable area and reinforced by the law. A state is not the same as a country. So, for example, England is a country but is part of a bigger state, the United Kingdom of Great Britain and Northern Ireland. Note also that the state is not the government; the government is a part of the state.

The government can be seen as directing what the state does in terms of policies and legislation but it is only a part. Defining the state makes it appear quite straightforward but the state, like the family are both quite slippery concepts. I often find that describing a social concept as slippery is useful because many concepts are sort of hard to really pin down. As a social science student you have to get to get used to this. You need to recognise concepts as being potentially slippery in that an absolute, or definite description, can sometimes be a bit elusive.

So, defining the family is not so easy yet it is something that we very often take for granted. Family is one of those terms that seems to be so obvious. You won't find it difficult to find texts which compare and contrast sociological theories of the family, Frost (2011) and Steel et al. (2012) are both very useful books (the details of all references are in the reference list below. Treat the reference list as a directed reading list and use it). Both books provide an insight into how the family has been explained from a sociological perspective, something which this book does not do. Frost (2011: 34) provides a useful table which summarises the positions adopted by 5 theoretical positions: Functionalism, Communitarianism, Marxism, Family Practices, and Feminism, in respect of how they understand the way that the family is organised, and this is a good summary.

In this book I am less concerned with how we might explain what the family does and more concerned in considering what we mean by the family and the ways in which the family is impacted upon by actions that are taken by the state. I am also concerned though what this means for children. This means considering the ways in which social policies are able to shape family life or experiences. Because of this it is important to come up with a workable definition or model of what we mean by the family.

We can see how the concept or idea of the family is embedded within UK culture but once we start to try to pin it down we run into problems. We can point to the idea of the nuclear family as an adult couple with children and compare this to an extended family, the same adult couple with children who are in a close relationship with other relatives such as grandparents, aunts and cousins etc. Although the idea of the nuclear family and the extended family are in everyday use they have real limitations in explaining what a family is because there is simply so much diversity. We can see this in the books that we read about families and in our own lives.

Although the nuclear family comprised of a heterosexual couple with 2.4 kids features very strongly in ideas about families we know from our everyday experiences that many families do not look like this. We can identify single-parent families, reconstituted families, same-sex families, and others and in doing so, recognise that families come in a variety of forms. Importantly though how those forms are understood can be important. For example, Shaw et al. (2013) introduces the idea of 'satellite' and 'multi-local' families which come about when one adult family member works a long distance from the family home. This entails setting up a second home. We should keep this in mind when we think about workers who move to different countries for work not only in terms of workers who may work a long way from their UK home and family.

It may be more useful then to move beyond trying to pin down an unambiguous definition of family by recognising that family can be seen as both singular and plural, (Morgan et al., 2019). So, each family may differ in terms of form but it still corresponds to what we refer to as family. Of course we might then think about just what it is that makes it a family. Morgan et al. (2019) is good for this in respect of how they point to three important characteristics: dependency, mutuality, and obligations.

Think about how, within a family, we can often pick out the ways in which relationships exist in ways which reflect dependency and responsibilities, mutual interests or concerns and a sense of obligation to others because of who they are. If we take this approach then we move away from the sort of approach whereby we have an idea or model that we then measure or compare others against to see if they fit the model or not. This gives us a much more fluid approach.

In recent years much academic research has come to be framed by this more fluid approach, the notion of family practices, a concept identified and outlined by Morgan (2011). In this model the family is what the family does rather than having to correspond to some rigid definition. As a theory this places a greater emphasis upon agency, our capacity to act. It is less concerned with structures or structural forces. Sociology tends to fall into one of two positions, either structure or action, action is often referred to as agency and you will come across these ideas a lot.

In its simplest form structure refers to large scale social structures such as how society is shaped by economic forces. From this perspective we, as individuals, are shaped by society. The opposite position is that of action or agency. In this perspective society is shaped by the actions of people. The action perspective is an approach which works very well in explaining social change and that is where I started this discussion, by referring to changes in respect of the family. With this in mind it is useful to emphasise a point that Morgan (2011) makes on p3 of Rethinking Family Practices, "there is no such thing as 'the family'". In saying this, Morgan is bringing diversity to the fore.

When reading this quote from Morgan you need to focus on the use of 'the' within the statement. Using 'the' always puts a particular slant on things and it's something that students often do, but very often shouldn't do. We call using 'the' in this way 'the definite article'. What we mean by this is that by adding 'the' we present the idea that there is only one, clear definition or version of whatever it is we are referring to. So, Morgan says "there is no such thing as the family" and he is correct. What we can't say is that there is no such thing as 'family'. Saying 'family' rather than 'the family' opens up the possibility of diversity. Think about this as you write your assignments and always be very careful how you use the word 'the'.

As a student, should you have an assignment that requires you to engage with the notion of family you might find Morgan's approach very good for talking about families in contemporary society. There are families but to refer to the family, as I do in the title of this book, is problematic. You can outline earlier approaches and refer to how they may be seen as rigid and then move on to say how the family practices approach put forward by Morgan (2011) is able to accommodate diversity and social change.

Importantly though, as I draw this section to an end you need to be careful not to assume that this more fluid approach that I have referred to is universally welcomed. From an academic perspective it is more accurate and it is more useful but that does not mean that it does not have its critics. One thing that often stands out in terms of academic issues is that very often ideas are contested. This can pose problems for some UK students as they have had years of being told that there is a right answer. Once you start a Higher Education course though you start to see that as very often, especially in social sciences, this is not true. There may be right and wrong ways of doing things but most of the time it is up to you to demonstrate why you are right and to do that you have to read a lot.

Frost (2011) is useful for illustrating this. Chapter 3 of Frost opens with a quote from Smart (2007) relating to the decline of the nuclear family and the rise of the fluid family. This is characterised by two opposing views: one from Morgan (1998) compared to one from CAVA. (Confusingly maybe, the Morgan referred to here is Patricia Morgan rather than David Morgan as discussed above. Patricia Morgan adopts a conservative approach towards families whilst David Morgan adopts a progressive approach. Do not get them mixed up! CAVA is a research group based at the University of Leeds. Their work is available online at https://www.leeds.ac.uk/cava/index.htm).

Frost presents these two opposing views as being able to be summarised as fear and concern versus appreciation and celebration. Almond (2008) provides a similar argument to Morgan regarding the ways in which legislation and social policies intersect with social change in being a threat to the institution of marriage. What both do is to reinforce the argument that is being put forward in this book in that legislation and social policies, things which are put in place by the state, act to shape the lives of children and families.

1.2   The things we do for love

So far I have been talking about families but we could also step back and ask about how families form. There are social and cultural aspects to this. Many of us will marry or live with a long-term partner in a monogamous relationship. Why? There is a strong emphasis in UK culture on the idea that we marry for love but this is not as obvious as it may sound. Pinto (2017) provides a good overview of ways in which romantic love has changed over time. What Pinto illustrates is how social and cultural behaviours may intersect with biological factors. There may be a biological basis to the feelings associated with love and attraction but how this plays out is social. Beck and Beck-Gernsheim (1995) in their book "The normal chaos of love", point to how romantic love has changed over time as, they argue, we have become more individualised.

The idea that we have become more individualised in our outlook can be linked to the influence of the political ideology that we call neoliberalism. This is because the ideology of neoliberalism has been influential within the UK for the previous 40 years and because of the way in which it promotes and reinforces an individualistic outlook on life. A fuller discussion of neoliberalism along with other key political ideologies is provided in Creasy (2020a) Family, State & Policy. In one sense it is a little too easy to say that the social changes that we see, such as a more individualised outlook on life, are down to neoliberalism. It's not really sufficient to say that neoliberalism explains this on its own because there have been other social changes which impact upon love and relationships also. We might consider how the changing social position of women also changes attitudes towards love and marriage. So, be careful with theory, neoliberalism provides a framework within which we become more individualistic but it may not be sufficient on its own to explain social change. It might be more reasonable to consider social change as a bit more complex and to recognise that two things, or even more, overlap and influence society.

Marriage on the basis of love is not historically or culturally universal. If we consider ideas about romantic love we see that a discourse exists regarding what love is and which may be read as a script. You may be wondering what I mean when I write discourse, if so don't worry. I will explain discourse more fully below. For now take the idea that I have just introduced, the idea that discourse is like a script in terms of how it directs what we do.

So, discourse acts to shape how we understand the world and this includes a way of organising our feelings and making sense of them within a particular social condition. It is certainly not natural though. To illustrate this let's say that you are a typical student aged 18 – 21. You have just started seeing a new boyfriend, girlfriend, partner. Think about what you might expect within this relationship with respect to your new partners behaviour towards you, or with respect to outings or gifts for example. Of course, you might not expect anything. That would be OK but talk to friends and ask them what they would expect or think back to previous relationships. You will soon start to see a pattern emerging which may suggest that there is nothing very spontaneous about love.

With an eye on gifts or outings, Mende et al. (2019) point to the ways in which romantic love is bound up with consuming things and services which act to define and reinforce the romance part of romantic love. Think of the common sayings "if you loved me you would..." (*insert appropriate act here*) or "isn't it romantic" as a term which signifies an act or thing as representing what is recognised or accepted as being romantic.

This is explained in an accessible way in Wilding (2017) in the text box entitled Focus 1.3 (p 10). Wilding draws on the work of Bauman, who I will say a little more about below, and considers the point that in a society dominated by consumerism, love becomes a sort of commodity. A commodity is something that can be bought or sold. It may be difficult to say that we can buy or sell love but think about how we buy what we want and that what we want can be influenced by how it is presented. Now consider the idea that we regularly engage in practices which commodify ourselves. Do we? Do you? After answering go and watch the currently popular TV programme, "Love Island" then afterwards, think about what I have just said about how we may package and present ourselves for a purpose and reflect upon the events in the show as following a recognisable script.

The aim of Love Island is, on the face of it, to develop a relationship and this returns us to something that was said much earlier in this chapter about how relationships are central to families. As such it may be useful to say a bit more about relationships.

1.3   Relationships

Relationships can be seen and experienced in different ways. With respect to the family, relationships used to rest upon marriage and were deemed to be long-term irrespective of what happened within them. We can how formal relationships act to constitute the nuclear family. We can now see different forms of family though. Remember what Beck and Beck-Gernsheim (1995) said about love changing as we become more individualistic. This involves a greater sense of reflecting upon what we want for ourselves. What we can say about this is that as we have become more individualistic so we have developed a greater concern with our own happiness and satisfaction. We start to see relationships as sources or satisfaction.

If you are in your teens or twenties you might find it useful to stop here and read this again but in doing so try to suspend what seems to be natural or normal to you. If you are a female student think about how at one time you would have been under pressure to find a man (ignore the assumption of a heterosexual relationship, we are thinking about the past) who would provide for you. Now think about what you might expect a man to provide.

I am writing this in early 2020. During Christmas, 2019, in the UK, the BBC showed a remake of a programme from the 1970s, Worzel Gummidge. Worzel Gummidge is very useful to students with respect to how he had the facility to change his head. So, if he was faced with a maths problem, he could remove his everyday head, and replace it with his maths head. What this enabled him to do was to look at a problem, or an issue, differently.

To be a successful student you will very often have to try and understand a problem or an issue from a different perspective. The sociologist Max Weber had considered this in the early 20th century. Weber said that it was important for sociologists to employ 'verstehen'. Verstehen is a German word which roughly means empathetic understanding. For us, the value is in terms of looking at something from somebody else's position; to look at something as though you were in somebody else's shoes. So, if you are 18 – 25 and you read that society has become more individualistic, that might be hard to understand for some because this is all they have ever known. In other words how society is now is perfectly normal so it is important to accept that it has not always been this way.

To make sense of verstehen then you have to try step outside of what you know and look at things afresh. Sociologists sometimes say that it is necessary to defamiliarize; by this they mean that you should try to ignore what you know already, difficult as that may be. So, by 2020 UK society had become very individualistic. It wasn't always like this, or at least not to this extent. Something changed and as it changed so our understanding and expectations relating to relationships and families changed with it.

At the same time what we might also see is that it can change again. The impact of the Corona virus pandemic during 2020 could lead to social changes which reduce individualism and see a greater sense of community cohesion. For example, consider how the period of lockdown had the result of shop workers and delivery drivers being seen as key workers. Consider how carers, traditionally low paid staff, started to be seen as important. This could, and I stress could, change the position of such workers in the future.

So, the way we live our lives, including social formations and/or structures such as the family is shaped by the effect of external trends and forces. Social change however, is associated with the loss of traditional certainties. For example, if we think back to the 1950s – 1970s the social world was much more stable. We tended to know where we stood in society and we could get a job for life. This was influenced by gender and it fed into how marriages and families existed. Our relationships within families were quite straightforward, certainly more straightforward than they seem to be now for many people. Saltiel (2013) provides a good overview of the complexity of some family lives with the term the "not-grandma" being of particular interest. The not-grandma referred to is a woman who provides care to a child and presents herself as grandma, but she is not a blood-relative.

You might also read what Zygmunt Bauman has to say about Liquid Modernity (2000) and Liquid Love (2003). I introduced the concept of liquidity above. For the idea of liquidity to make sense you have to take a historical view. For most of the 20th century UK society was much more rigid than it is now. Class, gender and ethnicity had much more of an impact upon how your life would unfold when it came to work and family life.

Although tricky at times the idea that underpins Bauman's ideas here is that the demise of rigid social structures and the rise of a focus on individualism has led to more fluid social practices. In many ways this is part of the normal changes of society. But, it may be worth considering that changes do not impact throughout society in an equal manner. Issues to do with class, gender and ethnicity can be seen to result in different experiences but there is more flexibility than there once was.

So, think about how changes in social context may create the conditions for different ways of understanding and for different ways of being, or doing, a family. In turn this will feed through into how children understand and experience the world. In relation to this it may be worth considering how situations are created where we are drawn into an increased concern with reflecting upon and working to establish, our identity. In recent social theory this has come to be referred to as reflexivity.

Reflexivity is concerned with the ways in which we increasingly monitor ourselves and reflect upon what we do and who we are. If you work in children's services you will very probably come across the idea of reflective practice. There's a subtle difference here in that reflective practice is concerned with reflecting on specific issues concerning the work role with a view to making changes and where reflexivity is a much broader and more general social approach that has come to characterise everyday life for many.

I often refer to reflexivity as a form of project management of our own lives. Think about how many people adopt a project management approach to life. Consider how we may reflect upon being a good parent or a good friend. Think about how many people may often take a significant interest in 'likes' on social media as though this is some sort of true indicator of who they are.

So, reflexivity is bound up with our understanding of who we are, especially in terms of relationships and aspirations. Wilding (2017) provides a good summary of the reflexive self in the text box entitled Focus 1.2 (p 8). Ferguson (2003) is also interesting in showing how individuals who are the subject of welfare services draw upon knowledge and understanding to influence how they are dealt with so as to secure outcomes that are favourable to them.

In conclusion, as the social world changes so this impacts upon families and family structures. Stable, long term nuclear families have become less common but the fluid family is much less certain in terms of roles and structures. It accommodates different forms. However, although we may recognise diversity, what we have already seen is that there may be resistance to this, and to the way in which society can be seen as changing.

In recognising that there is tension with respect to the family it is important to accept that this is because the family is not simply a term that is used to represent social relationships; the family comes to represent a particular set of values. However, in representing a particular set of values it can be seen as exclusive in that other values, alternative values are not recognised or that they are actively resisted as being lesser, inferior, or problematic. In turn this enables us to see the family as a site of cultural struggle, (Chambers, 2001). By this Chambers refers to the way that groups struggle to have their ideas accepted as legitimate or right. This is very often associated with discourse. Discourse also cropped up earlier so it is now time to make sense of what discourse is and what it means.

1.4 Discourse: Children and family as natural

As a student you have to read extensively, I can't say that too often. When it comes to discourse and the family Chambers (2001) is a really good book in showing how what we understand as the family is shaped and given sense as a consequence of the ways in which the family is presented to us. Chambers shows how we are provided with messages and images which define the family and this shapes how we understand it. Pause for a moment and think about the ways in which as soon as you hear someone referring to family a set of linked ideas regarding what the family is and does easily comes to mind. Now consider that the term family acts to focus what you are thinking about and that it makes a particular model of the family appear to be the norm.

Chambers focuses on the media and how the media provides a particular, you could say limited, view of the family and how this type of family then comes to be the focus of social policy and legislation which, in turn, have the effect of reinforcing this particular model. How social policy shapes the family is covered in Creasy (2020a), Family, State & Policy.

In particular Chambers demonstrates that the family as we know it is regulated within a range of social practices but where the state plays a significant role in this. In particular though, the family: is understood within discourse. As a student with an interest in children and families you cannot avoid being confronted with the concept of discourse so it is very important to have a basic understanding of what it is and how it works.

Discourse is a concept that is strongly associated with the theorist Foucault though it can be traced back to the work of Saussure, (Inglis and Thorpe, 2019) and Levi-Strauss, (Jones and Bradbury, 2018). If you are yet to be introduced to discourse start by returning to the idea that was introduced above regarding the way we act as though we are following a script which acts as a set of rules. Think about how the script reinforces ways of understanding different scenarios or settings.

Now turn your attention to the language that is used in the script and how this may influence your understanding. Think about the way in which our choice of language can influence what we mean about aspects of the social world or the ways in which it is understood. Inglis and Thorpe provide an accessible account to the way in which discourses act as rules which regulate the ways in which we think about the world.

A good example of this relates to people who are poor and we can see how there is a long history of using language to distinguish between some poor people who are deserving of support or assistance, and others who are undeserving. When we start to use the language of deserving and undeserving we impose a particular understanding on what we see, or in terms of how we might organize support or help for the poor. What we also do though is to construct an understanding of those people that the terms are applied to.

Jupp (2017) offers a more recent version of deserving and undeserving in using the terms 'strivers and skivers' but he also refers to families being labeled as socially excluded, anti-social, responsible, or resourceful. In terms of discourse these labels or titles act to organize how we understand different families and they come to operate as rules which give the illusion that these are real descriptions. The overall result is that we come to see some things as normal and natural.

You have probably come across the term, norms. So, discourse establishes the norms which we encounter in studying society and which guide how others deal with us, (Smith, 2014). As an example of this read Moss et al. (2000) and look at how children are understood differently in the UK compared to Italy and how this shapes the ways in which we provide children's services. For Moss et al the Italian approach that is often presented as the Reggio Emilia approach sees the child as resourceful and creative. The UK, on the other hands tends to adopt an approach which casts the child as lacking or incapable, hence the title of the paper by Moss at al, 'The Rich Child and the Poor Child'. Similarly Lambert (2019) offers examples of discourse in terms of 'children at risk' and 'families in trouble'. Cain (2016) is also useful in showing how a discourse about morals comes to shape single-mothers by viewing them in terms of being workless.

You will be able to find many other studies and papers which draw on the idea of discourse to show how we understand aspects of social life within a set of rules constructed within discourse. Our understanding of the world then is influenced by discourses and therefore, alternative ideas are either difficult to accept at the best or even unthinkable.

You will be able to find lots of books on Foucault and/or discourse, I think that Jones and Bradbury (2018) offer the most accessible introduction to discourse. That said, one book which provides a good introduction and which is relevant to family life is Nicolson (2014). Nicolson uses the example of domestic violence to illustrate how meaning and understanding exists within rules that are created within discourse.

Most of us would accept that domestic violence is a social problem. What Nicolson does though is to show that it is only a problem in the context of a particular discourse of relationships as based on mutual respect and equality, where physical violence is seen in a negative light. In another discourse, one in which the use of violence by one partner against another was seen as being a normal and necessary aspect of relationships (think about arguments against making smacking children illegal) then we wouldn't see domestic violence as being a problem. So, discourse shapes our understanding of the world and makes things appear natural.

The key thing to focus on here is the idea of what is natural. Discourse creates the illusion of things being natural rather than being something that is natural. Read that carefully, even I had to read it twice when I was proof reading! I am distinguishing between something appearing natural, and something being natural.

Consider the following from Smith (1998), "Discourse constructs the topic. It defines and produces the objects of our knowledge." (p273). In saying this Smith is pointing to how we can only know the family or childhood within discourse. Wells (2018) talks about how pedagogy (a focus on teaching children) and psychology have been combined in a way which constructs children as objects because of how they are focused on a particular form of development. So, the language that we use has the effect of constructing the reality of our world. It has real consequences for us. For example think about how children are much more restricted in what they can do or where they can go now compared to 50 years ago and how this is understood in terms of the risks that children face, (Creasy and Corby, 2019).

We can see how a discourse of risk shapes an understanding of threat and how this overlaps with a discourse of parenting which promotes ideas about what it means to be responsible or to be a good parent, (Creasy, 2020b). The result is that parents restrict the freedom that their children enjoy because we 'know' that there are risks to our children and we 'know' what we should do as responsible parents. Importantly though the parents which do not restrict their children may then come to be viewed as poor parents and may find that they are subject to investigation or intervention by various social services.

The discussion of failing families that follows in chapter 2 is an example of how discourse is an important part of how we understand families. Discourse also provides us with an insight into why it is that the state may be concerned with children and families. How the state understands children and the role of families in children's lives is associated with the ways in which it understands one of the key concerns of the state, namely the governing of society. The state can be seen to exist in some ways as a mechanism or system for social organisation. Planning plays a part in this with respect to future needs. With this in mind think about how the state can be seen to have adopted a particular discourse of childhood that views children in terms of their future.

So, the way in which childhood is understood shapes the way that children are treated and the provision that we make for them. In turn this shapes the childhood experiences that they have and this has an impact upon family life. In Creasy and Corby (2019), Fiona Corby and I propose that we see children as falling into one of two positions, we either see children in terms of what they are now or we see them in terms of what they will be in the future. This can be summarised as seeing children as beings, or as becomings, (Wyness, 2012, James and Prout, 1997). To add to this I am going to say that in general the dominant discourse relating to children is that they are seen as becomings.

Within this discourse the child's future dominates especially in terms of what children should be doing in the present if they are to achieve a particular outcome. This can be seen in respect of the state or in terms of services provided by the state. For example, think about how often government ministers or schools talk about children in terms of achieving their potential. Consider the way in which children's development is seen in terms of milestones and how not reaching particular stages comes to be a cause for concern, (Fattore et al., 2007). Milestones reflect the way in which childhood has come to be dominated by the ideas put forward within theories of developmental psychology and which has had significant influence in terms of constructing an understanding of children as becomings, (Walkerdine, 2009).

It is also possible to see how the influence of neoliberalism sees the education of children being presented in ways which promote the idea of educational success providing social and economic advantages for children in later life. In this way when potential is being referred to in terms of discussions about children it is not just in relation to the potential to achieve certification through educational success; it is also the potential to be economically successful in adulthood.

The alternative discourse of childhood is that children should be seen as beings. This is rooted within a more recent sociology of childhood. This position presents the child as being important in their own right. It is concerned with the child as they are rather than the child in terms of what they will become. Although this is a view that is much more common in academic discussions we can see how it has had some impact upon practice with children. For example, you may be familiar with the idea of the child's voice and with growing concerns that the child's voice should be heard. What we have to note here is that although this has come to be seen as quite normal it is not something that would have been recognised in practice even 30 years ago.

The fact that we identify these two basic approaches demonstrates that discourses compete and it points to the idea that was raised above that discourses make some things possible and other things not possible. Discourse then should be seen as a form of power. It is not physical power. It is not something that forces or coerces us to behave in a certain way. Instead, discourse shapes behaviour because of the way that it makes things seem natural, the way that things come to be viewed as unquestionable. Once we accept something as being natural, as being common-sense, we generally stop questioning it.

1.5   How might you use this chapter?

In reading chapter 1 I hope that you will have found it useful in terms of understanding changes with respect to families and relationships but at the same time you may also be thinking about how useful this is for you in terms of the assignments that you will inevitably be faced with. As a student it may well be the case that you find academic discussions about children and families interesting but you cannot avoid being drawn into assessment at some point. Assessment is a fact of life for students and it doesn't matter what you know or understand, how you perform in assessments becomes the measure of your ability. This is not to say that I agree with this, I see this as a rather limited or restricted approach. But, with the importance of assessment in mind this section will try to identify key points from the chapter and to provide ideas as to how you might use this in an assignment.

So, in terms of the family there are some key points which I would certainly expect you to be mentioning or considering within an assignment:

- The family is a key concept within social life but it is not as unambiguous or as clear cut as we may often think;
- We can talk about the family as singular and families as plural;
- The Family Practices approach provides a good way of understanding the fluid nature of families in contemporary society;
- Stable, long term nuclear families have become less common but the fluid family is much less certain in terms of roles and structures;

- We may assume that romantic love is normal but we haven't always formed relationships or married for love;
- The changing social position of women in society influences attitudes towards love and marriage;
- Children tend to be seen as becomings, in terms of their future, rather than as beings;

So, let's imagine that you have been given an assignment whereby you are required to discuss the family in contemporary society. This wouldn't be unusual on any course related to childhood, children and families, or a course related to working with children and families. You might choose to follow the basic structure of this chapter but you could also mix it up a bit. For example, you might use the section of discourse much sooner than I did. I dropped it in at the end because most students reading this want to read about the family not about a key concept within social theory.

OK, you are writing about the family. It makes perfect sense to always establish the key concepts early in an assignment. If the assignment is about the family you could open with a critical comment to state that 'the family' is an insufficient term. That is what I did. I started by commenting upon how the family is embedded within our ideas about society but then made the point that not all families are the same. I made use of theory by drawing upon Morgan (2011) and promoting family practices as a good way to make sense of what a family is. As Morgan states, from the family practices approach, the family is what the family does. I did say though, that although this approach works well in explaining family diversity there are some who resist the move towards the acceptance of diverse family forms. From a conservative position, change is not good.

I then used section 1.2 to question where families come from and used this section to think more carefully about some ideas that we take for granted, in particular, romantic love. I did this because I wanted to provide a critical understanding. I wanted to show that families are socially constructed and that what we might take for granted now has not always been the case. To help me I commented upon how the social conditions that we live in shape how we live our lives and what we expect. Section 1.3 is where I did this. Look at how I comment on the changing social position of women and what this means for relationships. I dropped a bit more social theory in by referring to Bauman and his concept that society has become more liquid. Tutors will always like to see you using theory in your work as this will demonstrate that you are providing an academic discussion so for all assignments think about theory and what it can do for you.

I developed theory further by writing quite a bit about discourse and showing that our understanding of families and the social experiences that we have are rooted in discourse. Discourse makes sense of what we experience. It makes things seem normal and natural. The example I used here is children. That made sense because the book is about children and families. So, I made the point that the social position of children and how we understand them is shaped by a discourse which positions them in terms of their future. If the focus is on children's future then that has meaning for how families operate. So, you could follow this structure and use this final point to say that although families may be diverse very often the way in which children are understood is very much shared and this means that there are some things about families which seem to be universal. I hope that makes sense.

CHAPTER 2 PARENTING & FAILING FAMILIES

2.1 Regulating families

In chapter 1 I introduced some ideas about what we mean when we talk about the family, including how it is better not to refer to 'the family' but, instead to drop the 'the' and to talk about 'family' or families. This reflects the diversity of families which we see in contemporary UK society. It also reflects the changing nature of society itself. In thinking about the changing nature of society it often makes sense to consider the role or influence of the state and although we often see the Government as being the state you do need to recognise that they are not the same. The state is much broader than the Government. Considering the state is important because it is the state which sets the context within which individuals and families live their lives. The state has power and this power can be brought to bear upon families in ways which regulate how they live.

Understanding the actions of the state as regulating families is a good way of considering what the state does as this refers to a way of acting upon families which may not involve direct or immediate force. Instead regulation can be seen as actions which have the effect of encouraging, coercing or guiding families. That is not to say that the state never acts forcefully but for most of us it is more a sense that we comply with the state or fall in line with what the state wants, often because we have no choice. This raises a question though; what does the state want? It could raise the question; how does the state come to want anything?

This returns us to thinking about how the Government can be seen as the driving force of the state. As such the Government is made up of individuals who want to achieve certain things for society. What they want to achieve can be seen to reflect their collective agreements regarding the benefits of particular political ideologies.

Political ideologies will also be discussed in Creasy (2020a) Family, State & Policy in much more detail. For now it is sufficient to accept that the government shapes the context of the state and that governments are influenced by ideas about what society is or should be and that this in turn sees governments introducing social policies and legislation which have a real bearing on the lives of children and families.

For example, the Labour Governments 1997 - 2010 were very concerned about what they termed 'anti-social behaviour'. This is behaviour that may not be illegal but which can be a nuisance for others who have to experience it. Alongside this they argued that very often a small number of families in a community could make the general life of the community poorer by engaging in behaviour that was anti-social, (Garrett, 2007).

One policy programme that they set up to tackle this was the Intensive Family Support Programme, (IFPS). This is a good example of how the state may act in ways which regulates behaviour because as Nixon (2007) notes "IFSPs do not solely contain and control behaviour, they also seek to transform 'anti-social' subjects into active, self-governing, responsibilized citizens." (p548). Nixon (2007) is a response to a critical discussion about the Intensive Family Support Programme by Garrett (2007) so it's worth reading both.

The term 'responsibilized' seems a bit of a mouthful and it might seem odd at first reading. What it means is that these families will have come to recognise that they have responsibilities to others. This fits very well with New Labour's concerns about rights being associated with responsibilities, (Driver and Martell, 1998, Guardian, 2002) but it also echoes neoliberal ideas about being self-reliant, (Cain, 2016).

Garrett (2007) is a very useful read in relation to how the state may act towards families because he shows how the state has set up policy programmes aimed at changing family behaviours in a number of countries, something that can be seen both geographically and historically. For example, as well as in the UK this includes the Netherlands in the 1950s and Nazi Germany in the 1930s. These examples reflect the actions of the state to stop families behaving in certain ways but policies can also be used to encourage types of behaviour.

Consider the New Labour policy of the Working Families Tax Credit. This was clearly a carrot to get parents in to work. It was embedded within the idea that there was a need to tackle child poverty and that getting parents in to work was the best way to do this. A more contemporary example of the state regulating family life is provided by Walker (2020) who illustrates how some countries are providing financial incentives for families to have more babies as a consequence of concerns about falls in population.

When we think about how the state often responds to problematic behaviour we may think of the ways in which the law is used and how offenders may be subject to forms of punishment. What the IFPS aimed to do was to support families so as to change ways of behaving rather than to punish particular events.

A similar approach was evident in compulsory parenting orders. Compulsory Parenting Orders were introduced by Labour for parents whose children were demonstrating problematic behaviour to the extent that parents found themselves in court. The orders required attendance on parenting programmes with the view that changing parenting would change children's behaviour, (Holt, 2010) something that will be considered further below.

What stands out in any consideration of the relationship between children, families and the state then is that the state can be seen to have an understanding of what children and families should be, what they should do and/or what they need. The issue of responsibilities introduced above plays a big part in this and it is under the New Labour governments of 1997 – 2010 that parenting started to take on a much more substantial role in terms of what the state expects to happen within families, (Lewis, 2011).

Importantly, it is by setting out a view of what responsible parents do that the state is able to be much clearer when it talks about families that are considered to be failing. Later in the chapter I will argue that this has overlaps with the idea of there being an underclass; a social class that tends to be associated with relying on welfare benefits. The next section however says more about parenting.

2.2 Parenting

There is a sense in which parenting can be seen as natural. We have children and we take care of those children; that is parenting. However, in recent year's concerns about the ability, or even the inability of parents to parent, has become very common. Parenting as a term is so obvious it may go without any scrutiny but as students of childhood and/or families it is always useful to be precise in stating what we mean. As such the definition given by Hoghughi and Long (2004) is a useful starting point. They refer to parenting as 'purposive activities aimed at ensuring the survival and development of children' (p5). If we adopt a critical approach however we might recognise that this definition is somewhat limited. I will say more about what we mean when we say a critical approach in the final section. The thing is, children will survive and they will develop within a wide range of conditions. In recent debates about childhood it is the question of how children develop, and the role of parents in ensuring that children develop in a socially acceptable way which is often the main issue. For example, we can see evidence of the state being concerned about how parents parent in the introduction of parenting programmes and/or parenting orders.

As this section is concerned with parenting, and in particular, the ways in which parents may be supported it is useful to establish what we mean by parenting programmes. Whittaker and Cowley (2012) state that "parenting programmes (social interventions designed to increase parental knowledge, skills and self-belief in their own capabilities in raising children) are key components of wealthier nations' strategies for the prevention of child maltreatment and improvement of life chances", (p138).

The Labour government's that were in power between 1997 – 2010 oversaw a number of parenting programmes being introduced and promoted. Sure Start Children's Centres played a key role in supporting parenting with named programmes being used in some cases such as: Incredible Years, Triple P, Strengthening Families Strengthening Communities, and Parent Gym, (Lindsay et al., 2019, Lindsay et al., 2011). In a study of parents who were on, or had been on, parenting support classes Corby (2015), points to the ways in which parents saw these as positive and beneficial.

However, what parents do is always within a social and political context. One aspect of the social and political context that is very important has already been raised though not explained fully; that is, the impact of neoliberalism. Neoliberalism is often said to promote the idea of individualism. By this I mean that we, as individuals, are seen as being responsible for our lives. If we are parents it is not unreasonable to extend this idea to a sense of responsibility regarding our children's lives. This includes our successes and failures.

This is a good example of how different social issues overlap. We live in a society that is unequal, and which is becoming more unequal. At the same time neoliberalism presents inequality as the outcome of individual choices and abilities. One explanation for being successful in life, and which rests upon an individualistic base, is the idea that some of us are more aspirational. We want success more than others and therefore we will work harder for it. Although this is a poor theory it is one which tends to be drawn on quite a lot so let's consider how this might feed into issues concerning parenting.

To start though it may be useful to consider that we can distinguish between the concept of parenting, and a concern with parenting as reflecting the ability of parents to control their children and to ensure that their children display appropriate social behaviour. This concern with control is not particularly new. Gorer argued that in the early 1950s, the development of a "tough love style of parenting had been the agent that changed England from a century's long tradition of brutality" (Field 2010: 18). Field however, has raised concerns that parents are no longer practising 'tough love' and considers that this has contributed to social problems.

Field (2010) is important with respect to how we understand parenting. He comments upon the actions of parents and considers how what parents do has an impact upon children. This is echoed by Allen (2011) in a report promoting early intervention. Allen states that: "What parents do is more important than who parents are" (xiv). This idea mirrors the idea that was raised in chapter 1 regarding what a family is and the development of the family practices approach in some ways. You will remember that for the family practices approach, the family is what the family does. In turn this accommodates the diversity that we see in contemporary society.

Mullin (2012) provides a useful discussion of the relationship between children and adults in contemporary society and introduces the idea of being a social parent as distinguished from being a biological parent. It is worth considering that to become a biological parent is quite easy, but it is also important to use Mullin's discussion to draw the distinction between being a parent and parenting. A parent may not demonstrate parenting just as parenting may be carried out by someone who is not a parent.

A concern with what the family does, and how they do it, is also central to the work of Lareau (2011). Lareau is an influential figure in how we understand parenting arguing that, in America at least, there are clear differences between how parents parent. These differences reflect differences in the social class of the families. As such Lareau argues that middle class parents engage in what she calls concerted cultivation. This is compared to working class families who, she claims, adopt a parenting strategy which she calls the accomplishment of natural growth.

Concerted cultivation is a style of parenting that is actively engaged with their children's education and development. If concerted cultivation represents 'hands-on' parenting natural growth reflects parenting that is 'hands-off'.

In the UK Lareau's identification of two types of parenting underpins the Effective Provision of Pre-school, Primary and Secondary Education Project (EPPE). The researchers behind EPPE however refer to active cultivation and place more emphasis on types of parenting than they do social class. In echoing Allen EPPE also argue that it is what parents do that is important rather than their socio-economic position, (Siraj-Blatchford et al., 2013). From this position social structures, such as class, and the social conditions in which families live take second place to the actions of parents and how they parent. This reflects neoliberal ideas about the importance of being active in terms of taking responsibility for our lives (Simpson et al., 2015), and in the way that the social context is ignored or seen as less important. This is a good example of an issue which illustrates the way that neoliberals view social life. As such we are left with the idea that good parenting is parenting that reflects the idea of active cultivation but where any consideration of the conditions under which families live is not taken into consideration.

A range of commercial enterprises can be seen to have developed to support the active cultivation approach providing activities which emphasise the long-term benefits for children. Such activities not only reinforce active cultivation as good parenting they also reinforce an understanding of children as becomings and as being a project that good parents actively manage (Vincent and Maxwell, 2016).

When you read Lareau, or writers who use Lareau you will inevitably come across the idea of the cultural logics of parenting. The term 'cultural logic' is rarely explained yet for students it is one of those things that really does need explaining. The idea behind cultural logic is quite straightforward if you start by accepting culture as referring to shared social practices. So, cultural logic refers to the patterns of behaviour and acting within a cultural group.

So if that is part one of making sense of the term, cultural logics we now need part two, the logic part. Logic refers to how we reason, how we draw on what we know and how we make sense of the things that we experience as rational. If we then identify ways in which the cultural practices of working class parents differ from those of middle class parents we start to see the idea of cultural logic reflecting each group's social experiences and understandings.

So, concerted cultivation, or active parenting is a rational and reasoned approach to understanding that can be identified as being located within a cultural group which in this case is middle class parents. This can be compared to a rational and reasoned approach adopted by working class parents that is different and which leads to different outcomes in terms of how they parent as it reflects the idea of natural growth. For each group of parents though, what they do, and how they understand what they do, is perfectly logical, both are rational and reasonable in relation to their cultural position and experiences within society.

Wheeler (2018) provides a good account of how Lareau has influenced thinking about parenting and has also demonstrated some weaknesses with Lareau's work. This is not to say that Lareau has no merits. Wheeler draws attention to some of the problems in using social class as a descriptor in 21st century Britain.

Social Class is no longer as obvious as it once was and because of this it is not so easy to just suggest that what Working Class parents do is different to what Middle Class parents do. What Wheeler adds is a way of seeing social class as a continuum and where parenting may change along that continuum. Note that Wheeler refers to 'essential assistance' rather than natural growth. The problem with natural growth is that it maybe suggests that these parents don't do anything at all and that would be inaccurate; they do the essentials.

This concern with how parents' parent is both important and relevant because a further aspect related to parenting that has emerged in recent decades is the idea that parents should be involved in raising the aspirations of their children.

What we start to see then is that in recent decades society has come to expect parents to play an increasing role in the lives of their children. This can go too far as in the case of helicopter parenting (Creasy and Corby, 2019). Helicopter parents can be said to intervene excessively but this can be understood in terms of the increased pressures that are brought to bear on parents with respect to their responsibilities towards their children.

However, parents need not be alone. It has become expected that parents should get some support in terms of their parenting though sometimes for different reasons. For the Labour government's 1997-2010 an extensive system of parenting support was established through the Sure Start system as first raised in chapter 1 and commented upon above. "New" Labour as they were referred to during this period drew on the political ideas of communitarianism, an approach which emphasised a need for a relationship between rights and responsibilities (no rights without responsibilities) alongside the benefits of strong communities, (Parton, 2006). This message was presented as a response to the individualism of the Conservative government's from 1979-1997, a time when Margaret Thatcher famously said, "there is no such thing as society, there are only individuals and families", (Thatcher, 1987).

What Thatcher's neoliberal message does is to reinforce the idea that we have no responsibilities towards anyone else other than ourselves and our families. As such you might recognise that it undermines concerns about communities. So, children are the responsibility of their parents and families are seen as self-sufficient. It is important to recognise that it reinforces the idea that we should support ourselves. Labour responds to this by pointing to the idea that there are times when we all need support and that we will all do much better when there is support.

In some ways the corona virus pandemic of 2020 demonstrated the failings of neoliberalism and illustrated why a political theory which promotes self-centred behaviour as neoliberalism does only benefits some in society rather than society as a whole. Such an idea saw Labour doing much to support children and families and although the state had taken an interest in families previously this had never been structured in such a positive way before. It could be fair to say that Labour changed the landscape of parenting within the UK.

One reason for Labours concern to provide support for parents can be seen as a response to poverty in the UK. More will be said about poverty in chapter 3 but for now it is generally accepted that poverty often disadvantages children. If so then we can argue that by supporting parents they will be better equipped to address the needs of their children and in doing so they will be in a better position to overcome the disadvantage of poverty, (Field, 2010, Hoghughi and Long, 2004).

Although this argument has previously been put forward to make the case for ensuring that all parents have access to parenting programmes other reasons can also be seen. For example, very often, parenting programmes can be seen as part of a raft of measures which fall under the umbrella term, early intervention. One important argument in support of early intervention is that it addresses a range of issues that, if unaddressed, can become complex, and expensive, (Gillies et al., 2017, Allen, 2011). Early intervention it is argued can save the state money as well as providing better outcomes for children.

Although the growth in parental support can be seen as being attributed to Tony Blair's Labour governments it does have a long history. Tisdall (2017) considers guides for parents such as Dr Spock's and indicates how parenting has often been dominated by psychological theories. Health visitors have offered support in the form of 'Parent craft', as a universal programme for many years. Other organisations such as the National Childbirth Trust and other voluntary agencies have provided programmes for pregnant women with respect to the early care of infants. In general though, the provision of parenting programmes beyond the early years has typically been aimed at families deemed to be having problems with respect to managing their children's care and behaviour. The idea that some families are problematic however is something that that has recently been presented as being the idea that some families fail.

2.3 Failing or troubled, families

The idea that some families fail has a long history. It is an idea that seems to have engaged a number of Governments. Consider the following quote from Tony Blair, the Labour Prime Minister of the time, referring to the unborn children of lone mothers on the 31 August 2006,"There is no point pussyfooting ... if we are not prepared to predict and intervene more early ... pre-birth even ... these kids a few years down the line are going to be a menace to society." (Gregg, 2010).

Without disputing that some families are faced with significant problems and may sometimes appear to be struggling, when you read about failing, or troubled, families what tends to be seen is that failing families are nearly always poor families. A word of caution is required here. I am not suggesting that being poor means that a family will be problematic, not at all. What I am suggesting though is that when we start to look at families who come to be referred to as failing it is not at all unusual to see that they are families who experience financial hardship, (Rose and McAuley, 2019, Jupp, 2017).

Discourse, as was discussed in chapter 1, is rearing its head again here because the term 'failing, or troubled, families' sets the scene for how we understand the living conditions and behaviours of 'other' families. It carries with it the idea that families can be measured against particular standards and notes that not all families come up to the mark. However, we can draw a distinction between families who seem to have specific problems that are restricted to their own circumstances and families who come are deemed to be problems on a wider scale in that they impact upon the wider community.

You may have come across the TV programme Supernanny in which Jo Frost intervenes in the lives of parents who are portrayed as struggling with their children's behaviour. This represents the family with problems that we can see as private. Supernanny presents a particular view of families, one where her parenting techniques will provide a solution for that family, (Jensen, 2018).

As was suggested above though, in terms of parenting, there is a suggestion in Supernanny that all problems are rooted in individual families rather than in social conditions. This is not to dismiss Jo Frost out of hand, rather it is to encourage you to consider that the families which come to feature in each show are families where specific parenting behaviours can be focused on. For many families their problems are rooted in the social conditions of their lives. It is important to remember the issues raised in chapter 1, drawn from Jones (2016) in the book "Chavs". Jones reminds us that it is important to consider the social conditions under which families live as this may provide some insight into the general living conditions of the family.

At the heart of arguments about parental support as discussed above is the idea that when parents fail this leads to social problems. What is deemed to be problematic will, of course change and what is expected or what is deemed to be normal for families and for parenting, changes. There are times though when moral panics follow high profile incidents or more general concerns about dysfunctional families or social breakdown, which leads to state intervention into family life, (Frost, 2011). One such moral panic can be pinpointed to the claims made by David Cameron when he was a relatively new Prime Minister, made as a response to a series of riots which took place across the UK in 2011.

After the riots Cameron did much to locate the causes of the rioting to be within families which he deemed to be failing referring to 'troubled families', (Crossley, 2018a, Garrett, 2018, Hoggett and Frost, 2018, Parr, 2017, Welshman, 2013). In referring to troubled families Cameron is talking about parents that are deemed to be a problem for those around them. In this way the private troubles experienced within families come to be the public troubles that are the focus of state intervention, (Ball et al., 2016). This is nothing new. Historical concerns with problem families have a long history (Lambert, 2019, Garrett, 2018, Garrett, 2007, Welshman, 1999). The Troubled Families Programme can be seen as following on from the previous Labour government's concerns with families who experienced social exclusion and this in turn reflected the Family Intervention projects set up in Dundee by the Conservative government under John Major.

Lambert (2019) offers a good account of how ideas have changed over time showing how this has seen the focus change from 'Problem Families', to 'Children at risk', and now, to 'Troubled Families'. Lambert opens with a quote from a speech by David Cameron in 2011 that is seen to mark the beginning of the Coalition and Conservative focus on Troubled Families, one that is often used, "we've known for years that a relatively small number of families are the source of a large proportion of the problems in society', (p82). Not poverty, not a lack of jobs, and not social exclusion; families.

The response was to set up the Troubled Families Programme (in England only) to work with families, rather than individuals in families, so as to change their lives. Two very good papers, illustrating the approach taken within the Troubled Families Programme are by Crossley (2018a) and also (2015), see the reference list for full details. Crossley (2015) is easily accessed online.

The definitive guide to the Troubled Families Programme is provided by Casey (2014). Casey, who was appointed by the government to lead the programme, writes that the programme is:

> "...working to 'turn around' 120,000 families over the life time of the programme. To be eligible for help under the Troubled Families Programme, families have to meet three of the following four criteria:
> - Are involved in youth crime or anti-social behaviour
> - Have children who are regularly truanting or not in school
> - Have an adult on out of work benefits

- Cause high costs to the taxpayer

However for most of these families, such problems are often part of a much more complex picture where many other issues are at play. We have recently published a report - Understanding Troubled Families – which is based on data collected by local authorities of a sample of families who have been helped by the Troubled Families Programme. This showed in addition to the expected problems related to crime and anti-social behaviour, absence from school, and unemployment, that on entry to the programme, troubled families had the following characteristics:

- 71% of families had a health problem
- 42% of families had had police called out to their address in the previous six months.
- 29% of troubled families were experiencing domestic violence or abuse on entry to the programme.
- Over a third of families (35%) had a child who was either a Child in Need, subject to child protection arrangements or where a child had been taken into care
- One-in-five (21%) had been at risk of eviction in the previous six months

Families had on average nine problems related to employment, education, crime, housing, child protection, parenting or health on entry to the programme. This is based on those families for which full data were available across every problem (1048 families)." (p82).

Casey is understandably positive about the programme but more critical accounts are available and you are advised to read some of these. Fletcher et al. (2012) provide some explanations as to why they considered that the Troubled Families Programme was unlikely to work while Levitas (2012), Crossley (2015) and Jupp (2017) point to some major weaknesses in terms of the claims that have been made in respect of the programme (Levitas and Crossley are easily accessible online).

These authors are critical of the figures that the Troubled Families Programme is based on such as how the number of so-called troubled families was arrived at, and in terms of the success of the programme, something which Crossley refers to as 'unbelievable'.

One problem with the Troubled Families Programme is that it assumes that families have problems which do not change when this is not the case. So, a family where children regularly truant may find that they are recorded as having been successfully turned around on the basis that their children have left school, or where adults find work. However, in spite of these weaknesses, in January 2020 HMGovernment (2020) announced up to £165 million for 2020 – 2021 on the grounds that:

> "...compared to families with similar characteristics who have not been on the programme, 19-24 months after starting to receive support:
> - the proportion of children on the programme going into care has reduced by a third
> - the proportion of adults on the programme going to prison has reduced by a quarter and juvenile convictions reduced by 15%
> - more people on the programme are back in work, with 10% fewer people claiming Jobseekers Allowance.
>
> The programme was originally set to run for 5 years from 2015 to 2020 but was extended by a year in Spending

Round 2019. Today £165 million of funding has been confirmed for 2020 to 2021.

Since the current programme began in 2015, 297,733 families have made improvements with the problems that led to them joining the programme. In 26,848 of these families one or more adults has moved off benefits and into work." (n.p.).

What stands out in a number of the books and papers that you will encounter regarding problem, or troubled, families is an association with the idea that within society it is possible to identify a class of people who form a group at the very bottom of society. This has been called a number of things over time but since the 1980s it has usually been referred to as the underclass.

It is hard to explore the issue of failing families without considering how this overlaps or draws upon, ideas about an underclass. As such the following section introduces ideas about the underclass debate. Although you may never be asked to write an assignment about the underclass being able to write about the underclass in an assignment about failing families will inevitably make you look stronger.

2.4   Failing families as the Underclass?

The link between failing, or troubled, families and the underclass is evident in a number of books and articles. For example, in his book on a history of the underclass, Welshman (2013) starts by quoting from the ex-Prime Minister of the UK, David Cameron, referring to a need to sort out the lives of 'troubled families' as was considered above. Cameron is but one of a number of Prime Ministers who have expressed a desire to tackle the 'problem' of troubled families.

This is relevant because although on the surface debates about the underclass can be seen as being rooted in concerns about poverty, discussions of the underclass often focus on a particular type of family. Welshman makes the point that his book is not really "a history of poverty per se, but of a particular interpretation of the causes of poverty that has reappeared periodically under slightly different labels" (pp1-2). In many texts about the underclass such as Murray et al. (1996) or Neckerman (1993), the place of families is of major significance.

In some ways the 21st century concern with families who may be referred to as troubled, failing or problem families is the latest version of an enduring concern with poor people who are 'not like us', (Welshman, 1999). The rise of a concern with problem families can be traced back to the 1940s but it can be seen to have emerged at a time when previous explanations which proposed that poverty was caused by biological weaknesses amongst some groups within society had become discredited, (Garrett, 2018, Macdonald et al., 2014, Welshman, 2013, Garrett, 2007).

Since the 1970s in particular the underclass has also been associated with the state provision of welfare. The Welfare State is discussed in the following chapter. Although the Welfare State was very successful in raising the living standards of millions of people in the UK there has been widespread criticism of it, particularly from what became known as the New Right (see Creasy 2020a for explanations of the New Right).

One of the main critiques of the Welfare State especially as put forward by the New Right (discussed in chapter 3) is a concern with the creation of a 'dependency culture', (Garrett, 2018). This refers to the ways in which people are said to become dependent upon welfare benefits to the extent that they cease to look for work and start to expect that the state will look after them. This overlaps with ideas about the development of the underclass.

Though hard to define, as will become obvious, the essence of the notion of the underclass is that of dependant 'scroungers' who have not only no desire to work but who also hold different values to the rest of society as characterised by the spread of single-parent families and of crime. Bagguley and Mann (1992) sum this idea up quite succinctly in the title of their excellent review of underclass theories, "Idle, Thieving, Bastards."

To make sense of the idea of an underclass though we have to accept the idea that society is stratified, or layered in ways which we typically refer to as social classes. Social class itself is something that is often debated but for now don't worry about what determines membership of other social classes, just accept that there are arguments which propose that there is an identifiable underclass.

For example, Runciman (1990) argued that there is definitely a class below the working class in the same way that there is a class above the middle class. This underclass constitutes those members of society who are more or less permanently at the economic level at which benefits are paid. Jordan (1973) also pointed to benefits as a decisive factor in defining the underclass calling welfare dependants a claiming class.

In contemporary society however it is a term then that is often used when referring to the poorest sections of society but in a very specific way in that it is used in relation to cultural issues. In raising the issue of culture I am considering how the underclass are often portrayed as living a particular lifestyle, or holding particular values which shape their behaviour. It is not simply a label that is applied to individuals who claim benefits.

For an example of this read Paterson et al. (2016) or Bom et al. (2018). Van der Bom et al (2018) analyse public tweets that were posted in response to the UK TV programme "Benefits Street series 2" and the way in which tweeters make reference to lifestyle choices, usually in negative ways.

In respect of the underclass there are two specific perspectives that can be taken to explain how it is formed:
1. Cultural: they create themselves. This is a right-wing view which sees the problem as the Poor themselves. Thompson (2017) explains this as a pathologizing explanation. By this he means that the poor have some personal failing which sees them as unable to escape poverty;
2. Structural: they are created by social structures. This is a left-wing view where the problem is the structural conditions which create poverty. In this perspective inequalities result from how society and the economy are organised.

The modern usage of the term, the underclass can be seen in Keith Josephs concept of a 'cycle of deprivation' (Page, 2015, Macdonald et al., 2014, Welshman, 2013). Sir Keith Joseph is important because he played a central part in the Thatcher governments after 1979 and, as a consequence, was able to influence social policies relating to poverty. During the early 1970s Joseph argued that even in a period of economic prosperity it was possible to identify groups who were living in poverty and claimed that this was being transmitted through generations. Joseph described this as a cycle, which continually acted to reproduce poverty.

This idea has become a common-sense explanation in relation to children and families as is illustrated by Simpson et al. (2015). Simpson interviewed early years' practitioners in a deprived town in the North East of England and found that it was not uncommon for them to describe their role as intervening to break the cycle of poverty. Respondents, that is to say, Early years practitioners, tended to accept a view of poor families as them not being aspirational.

This reinforces the cultural explanation of poverty that is seen in the arguments put forward by Joseph. There is a sense that Joseph is suggesting that children in some poor families were being socialised into accepting poverty, and a reliance on state benefits as normal. This is an idea that is very strong within popular depictions of poverty as being cultural within the UK, (Calder, 2016, Simpson et al., 2015, Macdonald et al., 2014).

The problem with this explanation however is that this is not usually the case, this is very generalised. Many people move in and out of poverty and this theory is unable to account for any significant transmission of intergenerational poverty. In spite of influential commentators talking about families where three generations had never worked as being a fact, (Calder, 2016) the evidence is very hard to find.

Macdonald et al. (2014) detail how they tried to find families where three generations had never worked by carrying out research in deprived communities in both Glasgow and Middlesbrough but failed. Glasgow and Middlesbrough are both areas where extreme poverty has been located for quite some so it was reasonable to investigate inter-generational poverty in these areas. However, although welfare practitioners in these areas would often talk about such families and the idea of such intergenerational poverty as being firmly in place, the reality was somewhat different. What stands out from all of the interviews carried out by Macdonald et al is a strong commitment to working rather than relying on benefits.

This focus on the family as a transmitter or socialiser of poverty though shifts concerns away from the structural roots of poverty such as the availability of jobs or the level of pay by blaming the poor for their own poverty. This is why it is termed a cultural explanation. It is an explanation which can be seen as underpinning the very influential work of Murray (1984). See also Murray et al. (1996).

Murray makes an important distinction in his work in saying

that he is not referring to the degree of poverty but to a type of poverty (though I would hasten to add that it may be better to substitute a type of response to poverty rather than simply a type of poverty). This clearly defines Murray's argument as a cultural argument. Arguments such as this can be seen to be adopting a victim-blaming approach in that they.

It is worth pointing that Murray's type of poverty is not really new nor does he claim it to be and he cites British poverty in the 19th Century to show this. Murray's type of poverty, the type that he sees as belonging to the underclass, is what we often hear being called the undeserving poor, the feckless, the residuum, (Welshman, 2013, Mann, 1992). He sees the people who form these groups as dishonest and distinguishes between the 'honest poor' (as he claims his parents had been) and the 'dishonest poor' who he is focused on. You might recognise a process of othering going on here.

Murray refers to the underclass as being the same as a disease and in talking about his work in Britain he set out to consider whether or not the plague (a term which he uses), which he has identified in the United States is spreading to the U.K. asking if we in the UK are being contaminated, (Levitas, 1998). Importantly though Murray argues that this plague cannot be cured by providing more jobs or by providing higher benefits.

This is because the people who constitute the underclass are healthy people of working age but who have a very different understanding of life compared to the rest of us. For Murray et al. (1996), they "live in a different world" (p26). Now, as a student you will no doubt have been told on numerous occasions that if we are to make claims, as Murray does, then we need some evidence.

The question then is what evidence does Murray have? Murray's original work relating to Britain is freely available online. Reading it you will see that Murray concentrates on three factors

which he terms the early warning signs:
- Illegitimacy (which Murray says is the best indicator).
- Violent crime
- Dropping-out from the labour force. (p26)

Taken together he argues that the statistical evidence of growth in each of these factors provides proof of the existence of an underclass in Britain:

> *"If illegitimate births are the leading indicator of an underclass and violent crime a proxy measure of its development, the definitive proof that an underclass has arrived is that large numbers of young, healthy, low income males choose not to take jobs"* (p38) though he also goes on to state that *"the young idle rich are a separate problem"* (p38).

Murray, then is arguing that the underclass are of their own making and as such his argument is clearly a cultural argument. Members of the underclass don't want family responsibilities or jobs, just benefits and easy money. The underclass has developed in response to high benefit levels, easy access to council housing and a reluctance to punish criminals. This is presented as being understandable, such a lifestyle is obviously very attractive. Who wouldn't want free money, cheap housing and not to be punished if you do anything wrong? So, the underclass is a cultural phenomenon explained by cultural theories. Or is it? Remember that as a student you are usually asked to be critical.

Dean (1991) suggests that poverty can be seen to be something that is rediscovered as a social problem in certain periods, such as in the late 19th Century and the latter half of the 20th Century. When this happens then notions of an underclass based on cultural caricatures are also reinvented. By caricatures Dean means that exaggerated stereotypes are referred to in ways which are said to represent a group overall.

What Dean is saying then is that the argument that the poor created themselves is a defence that the non-poor use so as to defend a social system which creates inequality and poverty. As such what happens is that the argument is presented which states that the problem is not the system, the poor are the problem. They are different. This is relevant now because there is lots of evidence to show that inequalities in the UK are getting wider and the poor are increasingly comprised of people who are in work.

2.5 Being Critical and using this chapter

Before I consider how you might use this chapter in an assignment it is useful to think about how a focus on the Troubled Families programme offers some good opportunities to develop your skills of being critical. I have said elsewhere that it is important to be critical. Most students study for a degree with the intention of getting a job and a critical approach is a useful skill to have in graduate level jobs. Employers will value staff who can identify weaknesses in arguments and processes. It is by identifying weaknesses that we can progress. However, you do have to be clear about what being critical is. Being critical in Higher Education assignments is not just a matter of finding authors who provide opposing views. That just leads you to the type of essay where you write Smith (ref) says this but Jones (ref) says the opposite.

As an example of a critical approach locate and read the papers that were referred to above by Fletcher et al. (2012), Levitas (2012), and Crossley (2015) and think about how these enable you to demonstrate weaknesses with the troubled Families programme. In addition, consider how the Troubled Families Programme is a good example of rhetoric. Rhetoric can be explained as persuasive language. It is language which seeks to present a particular image of something but which doesn't really stand up to scrutiny.

As a student one good approach to developing criticality is to try to test what you read or hear as being either rhetoric or reality. So, given that I am writing this during the Corona virus pandemic think about the ways in which the government and the media constantly refer to dealing with the virus by using the analogy of a war. Think about how the virus is often presented as having the ability to plan and attack when of course, that is wholly unrealistic. However, in terms of a message this type of analogy is very persuasive.

In the discussion above I demonstrate how you can use academic papers or books to build up an argument which identifies weaknesses in the Troubled Families programme. You could use Levitas to question the methodology used in arriving at a figure of 120,000 families. A further approach is to consider the claims being made. For example, the Troubled Families Programme is introduced as being concerned with achieving social justice, (Crossley, 2018b). This seems admirable. However, it is an aim that I would call seductive; who wouldn't want to achieve social justice, the alternative after all is social injustice. Yet, as Crossley notes, there is nothing in the Government's proposal which actually states what is meant by social justice.

Now, in terms of being critical if, as a marker, I was to read something in a student assignment along these lines I would be much more confident that the student understands what they are doing and that in turn is likely to be reflected in the grade. As a student your task is to convince the marker of your work that you have read widely and that you understand it.

One thing that I have said previously, and which I stand by, is that as students, you have to be precise when you use terms. You have to make it clear what you mean when you use a term such as social justice. In proposing the Troubled Families Programme, the Government does not do this. That means that I ought to explain what social justice is. I find it easier to do this by starting with social injustice.

Social injustice can be defined as unfair treatment or discrimination. So, social injustice can be said to be present when the rights and responsibilities of individuals, groups or categories of people are not respected. This doesn't mean that everyone has to be equal or the same. Equality is not the same as treating everybody the same and diversity is not synonymous with inequality. Different treatment only becomes a problem when it rests upon ideas about some deserving better and some deserving poorer.

We have social justice when we are treated equally rather than experiencing discrimination, when our rights are respected and where we feel that our efforts are fairly rewarded. This has not always been the case and some may say that it is not the case now. An excellent book for exploring social justice is Thompson (2017). Being critical can enable you to investigate such claims.

So, there was a lot in this chapter, let's try to pick out some of the key points if you were required to write an assignment about parenting or about failing or troubled families. Let's just add the warning though that the term troubled families is politicised in that it is rooted within a particular policy response to something that a particular government sees as problematic.

- The state often intervenes to regulate family behaviours;
- We can distinguish between being a social parent and a biological parent;
- It has been argued that what parents do is more important than who parents are;
- Parents are often seen as responsible for ensuring that children develop in a socially acceptable way;
- How parents 'parent' can be seen to have changed;
- Different social classes parent in different ways;
- Support for parents has sometimes taken the form of parenting programmes;
- Some families are seen as antisocial, often being re-

- ferred to as troubled or failing;
- The state has focused attention on failing families;
- Failing families are nearly always family that are in poverty;
- Troubled families can be understood in relation to ideas about an underclass;
- Children within failing families experience obstacles to achieving;
- The actions of the state provides the context for family life, this may help or hinder families

This has been an extensive chapter and I have covered a lot ground but we can still pick out ways in which you might use this chapter to build up a focused and structured essay. So, assuming that you have an assignment on Failing, or Troubled, families, how might you go about it. If it was me I might start by establishing the central role that families are seen as having and then state something like "however, some families can be seen as failing". If I start with this claim I can then go on to say that there is evidence from historical and cross-cultural sources which indicates that the state can act to regulate family life. Note, regulate rather than control.

In terms of how the state might regulate or what they might seek to regulate we could use the example of parenting as covered in section 2.2. This lets us talk about parenting as a social role and comment upon how it has changed. We could use Lareau (2011) to do two things: firstly to introduce the idea of parenting reflecting social class and secondly, to make use of theory. If I'm going to say that parenting differs based on social class I need to support this claim and Lareau works really well. I might comment upon helicopter parents as being one extreme and neglectful parents as the other. That could work.

The structure in this chapter sees me providing a more focused consideration of failing families by focusing on the Troubled

Families programme. This provides me with an opportunity to support the claim made earlier that the state will intervene in family life. I can also show how this is shared by governments of different political persuasions. In this chapter I introduced the idea of the underclass and illustrated how influential this was but you might not have the space to write too much about this. If so I would provide a brief discussion but add a few references. If you don't have space to fully discuss something dropping a few references in can help to give the marker confidence that you know what you are talking about and it shows that you have read around the issues. If anything an assignment on failing, or troubled, families is likely to be quite focused so take note of your assignment guidance and don't go off at a tangent.

CHAPTER 3 ESCAPING POVERTY: SOCIAL MOBILITY & LIFE-CHANCES

3.1   Housing Matters

Towards the end of chapter 2 I raised the issue of inequalities and the ways in which children and families are supported. Think about what Dean (1991) was saying in terms of how the argument that the poor created themselves acts as a defence against a social system which creates inequality and poverty. What he means by this is that the economic and political system that is in place creates social structures which mean that some groups experience poverty. However, some of us, especially those of us who benefit from existing social structures might not want to hear that it is the system that is at fault so instead arguments are presented which point to those who are poor as causing their own problems. However, as Schweiger and Graf (2015) point out, this cannot be said to be so in the case of children.

In this chapter I consider a number of issues relating to inequality. It is generally accepted that poverty creates a situation in which those children who experience poverty are more vulnerable to not doing as well as they might. Poverty is said to hold back children in terms of how they develop. However, this chapter is not really concerned about the extent of child poverty, though that will be considered. In this chapter I am more concerned with social issues which are associated with poverty and inequality in general. In this opening section I will focus on housing to illustrate how the way in which the state provides support for housing can be seen as contributing to some of the problems which families encounter and how this can have a negative impact on children's lives. Following this I will consider issues concerning how children may overcome, or escape, poverty and I draw on the programme set up by Bronfenbrenner in America, Headstart, to illustrate how the state in the UK has also intervened to tackle the effects of inequality in a similar way, Sure Start and how this approach has been dismantled.

In considering how political parties position themselves with respect to the family it would be highly unusual for any political party not to claim that they support the family. Indeed, Royston (2017) argues that there is an enduring theme presented by the Conservative Party as being pro-family, something echoed by Gilbert (2018). However, a distinction has to be made with respect to types of family as there is a clear sense that not all families are considered equally.

Those families who were discussed in chapter 2 above, families who very often rely on welfare benefits for income have often been seen in a negative light and do not appear to have been supported well since 2010. How this has affected children and families is reported on by the Child Poverty Action Group, (2019) who note that the number of poor children who are living in working families has increased to 70% of the total number in poverty in 2017/18. This is important because there has been a long-standing discourse within the UK of poverty arising from not working. In recent years however in-work poverty has increased significantly in the UK as the value of wages has fallen (Lyndon, 2019, Hirsch, 2018).

Recent changes to the benefit system also contribute to poverty within families. For example, changes to benefits have led to the introduction of a cap on household benefits and policies such as the 'bedroom tax'. The spare-room subsidy, often called the bedroom tax, is a response to the idea that some individuals and/or families live in houses that are bigger than they need when measured in terms of a ratio of people to bedrooms.

This is not to suggest that this policy applies to everyone, it doesn't. It only applies to those individuals or families who receive support from the state in the form of housing benefit and there are a number of rules relating to age and gender. It has the effect of reducing the housing benefit paid to a family by 14% where they are deemed to have one spare bedroom and by 25% where they have two, (Bone, 2014). The policy aims to encourage such individuals and families to move to housing which corresponds to their family structure though it should be recognised that this rests upon housing with fewer bedrooms being available to move into. This is not necessarily the case. What is evident though is that policies such as the benefits cap and the bedroom tax have had harsh consequences for some families, (Wright et al., 2020).

What has been suggested by some is that since 2010 the British social security system, originally established to support families experiencing hardship, has been reconfigured to put individuals off claiming and to punish those that do, (Wright et al., 2020, Fletcher and Wright, 2018). When it comes to supporting families, the state can be said to have taken a punitive turn towards those families who rely on welfare benefits.

We can also see how parents can be coerced by the state to provide for their children in particular ways or face punishments. Parents who fail to send their children to school may be prosecuted and even imprisoned as a consequence. In respect of truancy though it is often the case that truancy is sanctioned by parents for a number of reasons which are not acceptable to the state. Policies aimed at families then often reflect an approach which stresses responsible parenting (see Williams 2005: 296).

In evaluating such approaches it should be seen how the family is being presented as the base for social life and in terms of the development of children. However, in all of the discussions above about children and families one concept can be seen as being strongly tied to the family, that of home. When considering children it is not at all uncommon to question the home life that a child experiences.

It seems inconceivable to think about family without also thinking about the living arrangements of that family and the way that a family home is central to this. Think about how many television and newspaper or magazine adverts draw upon the idea of the ways in which we turn a house into a home. The relationship between housing and home is important. Think about your previous experiences of school and consider how home-school relationships have come to be presented as being vital to promote children's academic success. In a similar vein, Murie (2016) notes that from a neo-conservative position the Right to Buy policy, as will be discussed later, was presented as a means of "supporting the family and providing stability", (p31).

So, in terms of understanding children and families, the issue of housing is important because of the way in which it provides security and stability. This links to the state because the state can shape the landscape of housing. Housing then is a good example of how the actions taken by the state regulates the lives of children and families because of the ways in which the state can shape our access to housing and in terms of the standard of the housing that is available.

The most extreme form of housing problem can be said to be homelessness. It is difficult to arrive at an accurate figure for the number of homeless people and a distinction can be made between those who sleep rough and those who manage to find temporary accommodation with friends and family, what is often called sofa-surfing. That said, between 2010 – 2015 the number of rough sleepers in England more than doubled, (McCulloch, 2017). However, as this chapter is developing ideas that were raised in considering failing families I will not focus on homelessness. Instead I will focus on the growth and quality of the Private Rented Sector on the basis that this type of housing is increasingly the only housing available to poorer families.

For me, growing up in the 60s and 70s, housing meant one of two things, either buying a home, or renting a home. Renting was usually in the form of a council house but it was also possible to rent a house related to an industry. Growing up in South Yorkshire meant that renting from the National Coal Board was very common for families where someone worked for the NCB. Many villages in mining areas had extensive 'pit housing'.

At one time this sort of housing was much more common and many towns would have housing originally built by companies for workers. Saltaire in Shipley and Bournville in Birmingham are examples of estates built for workers. Bournville is interesting in that there are no pubs in the community, this is because of the influence of Quaker beliefs. Port Sunlight on the Wirral is a similar type of model village built for workers. The practice of employers building villages for workers does not happen today.

The growth in council housing can be understood as part of a process of municipalisation. This refers to the way in which local authorities became much more involved in the provision of a range of social services, (Child, 2018). During the 20th century housing became a political issue and you might find it interesting to compare the Labour Party's historical approach to housing with that of the Conservative Party's by comparing Child (2018) with Davies (2013), see the reference list as always. Today, the possibility of renting a house from a local authority (council housing) is much less likely. By the mid-1970s renting from employers had also declined significantly.

Note that if you have to write an assignment which includes a consideration of housing it is easy to access data on housing which shows the changes over time. The government website is probably the best source, visit https://www.gov.uk/government/statistical-data-sets/live-tables-on-dwelling-stock-including-vacants. This will provide you with access to lots of up-to-date statistics which you can use to demonstrate and support arguments.

After the Second World War the state demonstrated the aim to ensure that decent quality housing was available to all. This can be seen in concerns about replacing slums and with providing subsidised housing to meet the needs of groups who were less able to buy their own home. Housing costs can be high so council housing was subsidised by the state so as to keep rents at an affordable level. This approach saw housing in Britain come to be dominated by either ownership or by renting from local authorities, council housing. However, from 1980, housing was subject to two key changes, both of which reflect neoliberal ideology. Firstly council housing was privatised through the selling off of council houses to tenants. This led to the overall stock of council housing being reduced significantly. Secondly, the Housing Act 1988, along with the introduction of Buy to Let mortgages saw a major increase in the availability of housing provided by private landlords. Housing Associations also became more important as Council Housing declined. Following these developments what we see in 2020 is a general consensus that housing, the thing that provides security and stability to families, is in crisis.

Given that the state has had a long involvement with housing matters it is reasonable to say that the landscape of housing within the UK is not accidental. It hasn't just happened. The state has been involved and this has real consequences for children and families. Consider the points made by Bailey (2020) with respect to renting from a private landlord compared to social renting, that is renting from the local authority, something that is very common now, and think about what this means for children and families:

> "...private renting in the UK, as in many other liberal welfare regimes, is distinguished by high levels of insecur-

ity, particularly in comparison with social renting. This insecurity was the direct goal of deregulation policies in the late 1980s as these were seen as a necessary precondition for attracting re-investment. It is potentially a more significant problem for lower income households for two reasons. First, frequent moves may disrupt social connections to family and friends which low-income households are particularly reliant on as a source of practical and emotional support. These connections are especially important for those with children, and lone parents most of all. For children, there is the additional concern that frequent moves may disrupt not only their social networks but also their schooling, with longer term impacts on educational attainment. Second, the subjective experience of insecurity may be more problematic for those in poverty. As their housing options are much more limited, the threat of loss of accommodation is likely to be a particular cause of stress." (np)

Bailey paints a picture of a type of housing that is very insecure and this cannot be good for either children or their families. How we access housing tends to be referred to as tenure and tenure is of central importance when it comes to assessing the degree of security we have in our housing arrangements.

It is therefore important when we consider stability in children's lives. In the early 20th century renting from a private landlord was very common but one reason for the decline in private renting after the Second World War was because both rents and tenancies were regulated by government. What this meant was that landlords were restricted in the extent to which they could charge or increase rents and there were controls on evicting tenants, (Coulter, 2017, Lund, 2016). Regulating rents and making tenancies secure works in the favour of tenants in that it creates stability. Tenants can be secure with respect to the costs of their housing and know that landlords cannot evict them unless they have very good reasons to do so.

It is important to be aware that such regulation is also as a consequence of the actions of the state. Landlords had not created their own regulations or restrictions; these had been imposed by the state to make tenants more secure. As Coulter (2017) makes clear though, during the 1980s and 90s the state set about deregulating the private rental sector with a view to removing this security. This was in line with neoliberal ideas about the provision of social services and was made possible by the Housing Act 1988, (Kemp, 2015).

The Housing Act 1988 did two things that had a real impact upon renting. Firstly it allowed landlords to charge 'market rents'; secondly it introduced 'assured shorthold tenancies'. These are important because market rents mean that a landlord can charge whatever they want for a property and assured shorthold tenancies meant that tenants only have security for a short fixed term, usually 6 months to 1 year. In this case the assurance is for the landlord rather than for the tenant. It is worth noting that in cases of separation and/or divorce it is usual for a parent to be granted the right to remain in the home rather than having to sell it if there are children involved. This is based on putting the welfare of the children first and is often referred to as a Mesher order. The children of a family who rent within the Private Rented Sector are not provided for in the same way when it comes to their welfare. As was indicated above an assured shorthold tenancy in the UK is typically 6 months to 1 year. There are no rights for tenants beyond the period agreed to upon first renting in respect of staying in the property. Thinking about being critical you have a very good example here of how children are not all treated equally.

Now, in itself, there is nothing wrong with the shift from renting properties from a local authority to renting from a private landlord. Across the world this type of tenure is very common. As a student your task is to evaluate what housing means for children and families. So, it is generally taken for granted that stability in a child's life is something that is good. In terms of health we can also accept that the quality of housing is important. We may also be concerned that the standard of comfort within a house is important. With that in mind consider the following in terms of how Bailey (2020) makes it clear that renting in the private sector is often associated with poor standards:

> "…as Kemp argues, the PRS is "a demonstrably inferior tenure for low-income households" (2011: 1020). The high costs of private rents can act as a barrier to employment or push working households into poverty. Poor PRS tenants are almost twice as likely to find it difficult to pay their rent as poor social tenants. In addition, the PRS has long been noted for its poor property standards and poor quality of management. As it has expanded recently, this has raised the average quality of properties but those in the PRS remain more likely to have substandard housing. Poor PRS tenants are as likely to struggle to keep their home warm in winter as poor social tenants, and both are worse off than poor owners and non-poor renters." (np)

Given that our concerns in this book are with children's lives the issue of housing is clearly very important. If properties in the Private Rented Sector are often poor, as Bailey indicates it is not surprising that such housing has the effect of being detrimental to some children, (Bone, 2014). Given that council housing was seen as a solution to poor quality housing that was typical before the Second World War it seems concerning, though maybe not surprising, that the growth of the Private Rented Sector has also seen the return of poor quality housing conditions. However, the practice of privatising council housing and of promoting the expansion of the Private Rented Sector was a political decision. It was done on purpose.

The decline of local authority housing, council housing, or what has come to be called 'social housing', was made possible by the Housing Act 1980. This was introduced by the first Thatcher government and is often credited with providing significant working-class support for the Conservatives in the 1979 general election. The introduction of offering opportunities to buy council houses for a significant discount was very popular with many council tenants. Council tenants had previously been able to buy their council house but only if the local authority was willing to sell it and many local authorities were reluctant to do this because of the demand that existed for such housing.

Importantly though although the Right to Buy policy is always credited to Margaret Thatcher it actually predated her time as prime Minister, (Murie, 2016, Davies, 2013, Jones, 2007). What Thatcher did in introducing the 1980 Housing Act did was to compel local authorities to sell council houses to tenants, at a significant discount (up to 60% for houses and 70% for flats) and to restrict the further building of council housing, (Disney and Luo, 2017, King, 2010, Jones, 2007).

Thatcher's stated aim was to extend the number of home owners in the UK and his did happen initially but it has since reduced and ironically, very many ex-council properties are now rented out by private landlords rather than by local authorities, usually at much higher rents and with far less security for tenants. For example, for families who receive housing benefit to help them access housing, Bone (2014) points out that "claimants in the PRS typically receive around 57% more per week in housing benefit than their counterparts in social housing", (p4). What is evident then is that by 2020 the increasing cost of buying private housing is putting this out of the reach of many young people unless they are able to be supported by parents and that this is driving more people into the Private Rented Sector. This acts as a sort of catch-22 as the high cost of rents makes it even harder to save sufficient funds to buy a property and traps many families in insecure, poor quality housing.

As has been demonstrated above, the Private Rented Sector as it exists now within the UK is unable to provide the stability and security that we are often told that children require. As such, any consideration of children's lives, and their futures should be assessed in a way which takes housing into account. If we are considering the extent to which children can thrive most of us will readily acknowledge that children need a good base to work from. As such we might consider that the housing that children experience will have some impact upon their ability to do well in later life. In this way we might consider that for some children, their experiences of poor housing may make it harder for them to escape the conditions of their childhood and result in them having an adulthood that is very similar to that of their parents.

3.2 Escaping the Underclass

A key theme within cultural explanations of failing families and the underclass is the idea that poverty is reproduced as a consequence of children being socialized into a way of life. One key weakness with this argument is that it adopts a deterministic position. As a student you should always be on your guard when it comes to being deterministic. Always avoid determinism. Basically, a deterministic argument rests on the premise that X causes Y. Here's an example, I can say with confidence that heating water will cause it to boil. I can say with confidence that increasing pressure on a pane of glass will eventually see it breaking. So, sufficient heat causes water to boil and sufficient pressure will break a pane of glass. But can I say with confidence that growing up in poverty will mean that a child will remain in poverty as an adult? Some will, but equally, some will not.

Arguments which claim that growing up in a poor family will lead to a lifetime of poverty do not stand up to scrutiny. This is often because there are just too many factors involved. It is reasonable to argue that it may be harder for a child who has grown up in poverty to become wealthy in later life but it is by no means certain that they will not, some do. Importantly though it is important to recognize the social influences on how our lives develop rather than falling into the trap of arguments which suggest that both ability and inability are hereditary.

This is relevant in a book on families because although we have to acknowledge that families provide the social and cultural context within which a child develops, at the same time a family does not establish the limits of that child's future.

You will often hear people say "like father, like son", or refer to families as being "all like that in that family", but are they? Are you a carbon copy of your parents? I doubt it (recognizing also that not everyone lives with their parents). However, even if you were a carbon copy, the environment that you live in is likely to be very, very different than that faced by your parents at the same age. This means that if you were a child living in poverty now, what you have to do to escape poverty will be very different and the obstacles that you face will also differ.

So, if we want to consider the possibility of a child who has grown up in a failing family, or in poverty, of escaping and doing well for themselves we also have to consider a number of other social and economic factors. The thing is that children can be socially mobile.

The idea of social mobility is really quite straightforward. It rests upon understanding society as unequal but where individuals can move up or down in terms of social position. We typically characterize inequality on a vertical scale. Think of a ladder where each rung represents a socio-economic position. When we say socio-economic we mean that the economic assets, such as income or wealth, that we might have, indicate our social position. We usually refer to this as social class.

Typically, in the UK Social Class has been considered in terms of upper class, middle class, and working class though in chapter 2 I introduced the idea of the underclass. Official statistics within the UK though adopt the National Statistics Socio-Economic Classification (NS-SEC), (Goldthorpe, 2016b). The seven-class version of this Class scale is as follows:.

"Class description
1. Higher managerial and professional occupations, Salariat
2. Lower managerial and professional occupations
3. Ancillary professional and administrative occupations* Intermediate
4. Small employers (less than 25 employers) and own account workers classes
5. Lower supervisory and technical occupations
6. Semi-routine occupations Working class
7. Routine occupations

* NS-SEC names Class 3 simply as 'Intermediate occupations'. We elaborate on this to give a better idea of the occupations included." (Goldthorpe 2016b: 90).

Looking at the categories it can be seen how this represents occupation because it does not include those who do not work whether that be because they have no work and therefore may be seen as falling into the underclass or whether they are those who are wealthy enough not to need to work.

So, if we accept that the social class of a child is deemed to reflect the class of his or her parents then a child who moves from one social group to another, up or down, has been socially mobile. Be aware that very often social mobility is spoken about as though it means moving upwards. That is not accurate. Social mobility can be up or down. The glaring weakness with the Registrar general's scale is where a child lives with two adults who themselves are in different classes! Typically the man's class has determined the household class. We could say that this reflects two things:

1. That heterosexual families have always been deemed to be the norm;
2. That men earn more than women (around 20% currently).

In terms of social class and social mobility you will probably come across the term, life-chances. The idea of life-chances is very important in terms of studying, or working, with children and families, (Calder, 2018). I explain life-chances much more extensively in Creasy (2020c), Wellbeing, Vulnerability & Life-chances, including a consideration of different abilities and life-choices.

There is an argument that the inequalities which we see around us are the consequence of the life-choices that we make. It is not a very good argument but it is quite common. Life-chances is the term that is generally used when referring to a person's potential to achieve the sorts of things that are typically accepted as being desirable. This could be in terms of jobs, or in terms of housing or other material things.

As a term, life-chances originates in the work of Max Weber, a German sociologist. What is implicit when we speak of life-chances is the recognition that children have different opportunities. These differences reflect their childhood environment as that provides either opportunities or obstacles to doing well in life. In recent years much has been said about life-chances, especially in relation to children where life-chances is often is used in relation to social mobility and education, (Munro, 2019, Goldthorpe, 2016b).

Goldthorpe provides a good account of why it is that education is not as important in terms of upwards social mobility as it is often said to be. Be careful, it is not that that education is not important at all, rather it is that education cannot explain upwards social mobility on its own nor can it explain why less intelligent or less educated children from higher social classes do not experience downwards social mobility to the extent that we might expect if class position reflected ability and merit.

To explain why this is we need to consider the role of the family. For Goldthorpe it is the actions of parents in higher social classes which give advantages to children with respect to both upwards social mobility and which act as a safety net ensuring that less intelligent children are less likely to experience downwards mobility. At the same time, social mobility is a consequence of social and economic conditions more than being a consequence of ability or merit, (Goldthorpe, 2016a, Wilby, 2020).

Government ministers in particular often seem to equate evidence of social mobility as being positive and to promote it even as being a valid goal. As a goal, evidence of social mobility comes to represent success in terms of the social policies that are in place and with respect to the type of society that we live in.

Social mobility is another one of those terms which I always see as seductive, who wouldn't want to have opportunities to be socially mobile, to be able to improve one's social position. The opposite of course is a society that is fixed, or rigid, a society where the class that you are born into is the class that you will remain in.

Both Calder (2016), and Reay (2017) make the point however that social mobility is not a solution to inequality. Reay in particular notes that social mobility actually only becomes important when society is unequal. There would be far less concern to be mobile if society was more equal.

When we think about the life-chances of those who experience poverty though, we tend to see them as facing problems that are particular to being poor. This positions the poor as different and although I will acknowledge that the poor face specific problems we have to be careful not to see inequality as representing a difference between those that are poor and those that are not poor in a way which sees the non-poor as sharing the same social conditions.

An analogy that was often used after the 2008 financial crash was that we are all in this together and during the Corona virus pandemic of 2020 it was often said that we are all in the same boat. These analogies only work though if we all share the same social position. We can start to see things more accurately when we replace boat with storm and then think about boats. So, we may all be in the same storm but some of us are in ocean-going motorized yachts and some of us are in open rowing boats and some of them are a bit leaky. It may be the same society but we don't all experience it in the same way.

A good way of illustrating why inequality creates problems for all of us is provided by Marmot (2015). See Bosely (2020) also for an update on Marmot's work. Marmot refers to inequality as a gradient with upwards social mobility being the actions of moving up the gradient. If we are faced with a gentle slope (a fairly equal society) it would be easier to move upwards than if we are faced with a steep slope (an unequal society). Think about walking up hills. It is easier to walk up a gentle hill than a steep one.

What Marmot makes clear though is that this is not just something faced by the poor, that is to say those at the bottom of the slope. It affects us all. It doesn't matter where we start. Starting half way up may mean we don't have as far to go but it is just as hard as it is starting from the bottom.

So, relating what Calder and Reay are saying to Marmot's gradient analogy, social mobility does not change the degree of incline in which case a focus on social mobility could be seen as simply a way of making inequality more acceptable by promoting the idea that those who are more capable will be able to avoid the worst consequences, that is to say that they will be able to escape poverty. If so, this sees society accepting poverty but becoming focused on how we can provide for some to escape poverty rather than working to tackle social inequalities in spite of the problems that inequalities result in.

Ideas about how education can provide opportunities for social mobility can be seen to influence the ways in education systems are established. In the UK there is a lot of support for selection in schools and this is often associated with calls for Grammar schools to be re-established nationally on the grounds that Grammar schools provide opportunities for social mobility, (Creasy, 2018).

The evidence for this is not at all strong and what tends to happen is that in those areas of the country where Grammar Schools exist they appear to achieve better results as a consequence of the way in which they restrict who they admit as pupils to those children who are academically stronger. In general however children from poorer backgrounds are not well provided for with the existing Grammar schools, (Andrews et al., 2016, Coe et al., 2008). Grammar schools may offer advantages to those children who are admitted but the system operates in a way that means that this will always be a minority of children. What the Grammar school system does then is to reinforce social inequalities. More will be said about inequalities in section 3.4 below.

I have already indicated that poverty is often accepted as being something that can harm a child's life and this is something which provides a further opportunity to consider how the state may shape the context of the lives of children and families.

Some politicians have demonstrated concerns to tackle what is often referred to as child poverty. As such the Child Poverty Act (2010) introduced by the Labour Government under Gordon Brown required local authorities to report on the extent of child poverty and to explain what was being done both to tackle it and to reduce it. Governments were required to use this reporting to help them to combat child poverty and, ultimately, to eradicate it. If you are concerned about child poverty then you may see the Child Poverty Act 2010 positively. That does not mean that this concern is shared by all.

The Labour Government was replaced in 2010 by the Conservative led Coalition Government and this in turn was replaced by a Conservative Government in 2015. In 2016 the Conservative Government introduced the Welfare Reform and Work Act. This did two things in relation to tackling child poverty. Firstly, it abolished legal targets in relation to reducing child poverty and secondly, it stopped requiring local authorities to set up poverty reduction strategies. A further issue in terms of the Welfare Reform and Work Act is important. From 2016, the Child Poverty Act 2010 was retrospectively renamed the Life Chances Act 2010. By changing the name of the 2010 Act in this way poverty is effectively removed from political consideration.

As such it could be argued that in terms of the Welfare Reform and Work Act 2016 the Conservative Government demonstrated that they were no longer concerned with discussing poverty in terms of what this means for children. Instead, the focus is now concerned with who might be at risk of experiencing poverty, (Dickerson and Popli, 2018). Calder (2018) provides a good account of what this change means for children. What it appears to do though is to work from the basis that poverty is a fact of life.

In some ways it may be, we have already seen that there are very often some families who experience poverty in any time period. The difference is that for the politicians who drew up the Welfare Reform and Work Act 2016, working to tackle poverty appears to have been scrapped as a political goal. Instead, the goal is to somehow to identify who may be at risk of poverty.

Think of it as a snakes and ladders board where the ladders provide upwards social mobility and the snakes can see us falling down, possibly into poverty. The Child Poverty Act 2010 can be understood as working to remove the snakes, or at least, removing those that dropped us to the lowest levels. The Welfare Reform and Work Act 2016 seems to be relaxed about poverty and is content to identify who might find it harder to climb a ladder. What this does is to remind us, as did the discussion on housing, that the environment that a child grows up in can have an impact upon their future.

3.3 Bronfenbrenner's socio-ecological model

Given that this chapter is raising concerns about the conditions in which a child lives this section provides an example of how we might develop a broad understanding of issues relating to children and families andr how you can frame what you what write about them.

The idea of framing is very useful. It is an approach which can help you be more effective as a student because it draws you into providing a focus for your work. So, when we say framing we are concerned with the general approach that you will adopt so as to explain something. Usually it refers to either adopting a particular theoretical approach to explain something or to focus on one particular issue.

So, in section 3.1 I used housing to frame an understanding of how families live and to show how the state has done much to change the nature of housing within the UK which has then resulted in real problems for some families. In this section though I use the work of Bronfenbrenner to frame an understanding of children's lives in a way which changes how we look at children and their development. In considering Bronfenbrenner though I will also provide an approach that will demonstrate that an understanding of the state is important if we are to study children and families.

Many students reading this will have encountered the work of Bronfenbrenner (1979) previously as Bronfenbrenner's work has been very influential within 21st century Britain. A consideration of Bronfenbrenner's ecological model of child development should also provide a good justification for considering the role and actions of the state in any study of childhood. For example, most students on an undergraduate course in childhood will encounter policy issues. Policy comes from governments and although I explain earlier that the Government is not the same as the state, it is a major part of it. The state and policy is covered in Creasy (2020a), Family, State & Policy.

Bronfenbrenner's work is often presented as being an ecological model. We need to be clear what that means and but then I will tweak what we call it a little. Let's first say that ecology is about the environment and what we are doing here is thinking about the environment that the child lives in. Children live in an environment where the relationships between people are important. If we accept that relationships are important then we can also see that relationships are a social phenomenon and so now it makes sense if we see Bronfenbrenner's model referred to as the socio-ecological model. It is based on social relationships and how social behaviours and services often combine to create the environment in which the child lives.

Bronfenbrenner is concerned with children's development and draws on the work of Vygotsky to move away from the typical psychological model of development that has been the dominant position in the West for quite some time. For example, pick up any book entitled Child Development and it will invariably be focused on psychology. Usually psychological theories focus on the child as an individual and that fits very well with western ideas about individualism. Vygotsky was Russian and you can see his ideas as having been influenced by the more collective concerns of socialism. This can be seen in the difference in the position taken by Vygotsky, who develops a social-constructionist approach, compared to Piaget.

The simplest way of seeing the difference between the Piagetian and the Vygotskyan approaches is that for Piaget, the child is like a little scientist. The little scientist explores their own world as an individual and make sense of it as they do so. However, as they explore they are constrained to a large part by the fact that, for Piaget, they go through stages of development. For Vygotsky, the child is more like a little apprentice. As an apprentice they learn about their world in the company of others, and are guided by those who are more knowledgeable. Grasping this is essential to make sense of Piaget and Vygotsky. Be clear about what the differences are but accept that this is a simplified version.

Now consider the culture in which each was developed, both were working around the same time. Piaget was working in Europe where ideas about individualism were dominant. Vygotsky was working in Russia where ideas about being part of society were dominant. When we think about it like this we can start to see how our ideas are shaped by our social and cultural experiences. For a good critique of psychological approaches to child development read Walkerdine (2009). Walkerdine is also good for demonstrating how certain ideas come to be accepted as normal within discourse.

As such Bronfenbrenner considers what contributes to the social and cultural aspects of how a child develops. He presents a range of influences that are usually illustrated as a set of Russian Dolls or, more usually, as concentric circles, where the child is at the centre.

So, taking the typical representation of Bronfenbrenner's model as being a set of concentric circles with the child at the centre, what we see is that the immediate concern is the child's world, the micro-system of families, schools and day-care settings. The child's peer group would be here. However, these settings are not independent of each other so changes in one micro-factor may affect the child in another. As an example of this consider the relationships between families and schools. This has been seen as being of importance for some time, (Siraj and Mayo, 2014, Knowles and Holmstrom, 2013, Whalley and Centre, 2007, Hughes et al., 1994). Not all families are supportive of the work that schools do. What this means is that a child in a family that we could call school-resistant may experience school very differently to a child living in a family that is school-supportive.

We can also see that a child is affected by settings which they are not involved in, exo-systems such as the parent's work place. So, if parents have to work long hours or have a job that involves shift-work we might think about how this could impact on children. As a child I can remember being told to be quiet whilst playing in the garden during school holidays because Dad was in bed, having worked a nightshift. Similarly, when I was in my mid-20s I remember going a week or so hardly seeing my daughter because I was working the night-shift (one perk to being a lecturer is that I no longer work night shifts!).

The next factors in Bronfenbrenner's model reflect the much broader elements of society and culture such as government policies, values, religious practices etc. What we should also recognise however is that a final system can be identified as the chronosystem. The chronosystem represents change over time. So, my experience of childhood will have been different to the typical 18 – 21 year old student's experience of childhood now because society has changed over time.

Bronfenbrenner is relevant because he presents a theoretical model for understanding the context of children's development which recognises the limitations of many psychological theories. He was also heavily involved in policy programmes which directly affect children's lives. This is the link to the state! Bronfenbrenner's work was the basis for the Head Start programme in the USA and was instrumental in shifting the focus away from the child in isolation, which psychological theories often do, to consider children's position within families, communities, and society.

The Head Start programme focused upon families and communities which are suffering disadvantage. The policy was based upon evidence which demonstrated that children from deprived backgrounds performed less well at school. The aim was to level the playing field. In the UK the Labour government from 1997 – 2010 drew from the success of Head Start in the US and introduced a similar policy programme which they called Sure Start.

Sure Start was also a programme aimed at overcoming the disadvantage that is typically experienced in poorer communities. However, although Sure Start was successful as a policy approach, (Donetto and Maben, 2015, Hall et al., 2015, Lewis et al., 2011, Anning and Ball, 2008) policy changes introduced by the Coalition and Conservative governments since 2010 effectively closed it down.

In considering Bronfenbrenner though my aim is to demonstrate why a consideration of the state is necessary if we are to understand the lives of children and families. If we consider Sure Start as an example of a state-run programme we can see why it is that any consideration of children and families also needs to consider the role of the state. This is because the experiences of childhood and children's lives, and their futures, can be seen as being shaped by the state. If we take a simple view of Bronfenbrenner's basic model, children's development takes place within families and this influences issues relating to how they develop by shaping their experiences and opportunities. At the same time the position of families is influenced by a range of issues relating to the state such as the extent of support that is provided to families or policies which shape the economic position of different families.

A particular focus within chapter 2 was a concern in the UK with what has often been referred to as failing families, or alternatively, troubled or even troublesome families. Such families are seen as presenting a problem not only for the communities that they live in but also for themselves. Think about this in relation to child development. Previously I referred to phrases such as "I blame the parents", or "the apple never falls far from the tree"? These sayings suggest that children will not only learn from their parents, they will grow up to be increasingly like their parents. So, this argument suggests that if parents engage in behaviours that are considered to be problematic we can expect their children to also engage in similar behaviours. Well, that's the idea.

It is not difficult to pick holes in this idea as I have previously demonstrated. This is not to say that children do not learn from their parents nor is it to say that they won't adopt some of their parents' habits or ways. I did say though that as a student you must always be careful not to fall into the trap of being deterministic. When we say 'I blame the parents' we are saying that children have no free will, no agency. In sociology agency refers to our capacity to make our own decisions and act on them. The argument that children will be just like their parents is also suggesting that children are only influenced by their parents and that is clearly not the case. Children are not only subject to socialisation from their parents, children are also subject to a range of influences such as from their peers, or their experiences at school and the influence of the media.

Bronfenbrenner's socio-ecological model reflects this aspect of children's lives and gets us to think about the range of factors and settings which shape the context within which children develop. To reiterate what Bronfenbrenner is saying though this all takes place against a more general backdrop of social, cultural and economic factors which are all significantly shaped by the state.

As an example read the book, Chavs by Jones, (2016, 2012). Focus on how Jones describes and discusses the changes that families in Ashington, Northumberland, have experienced since the decline of the mining industry. Many families in Ashington included men who worked in mining. That work has now gone and though some of us found other jobs many struggled to secure other work and some of these families may be more reliant on state benefits than before. Other sectors of the economy have also seen a decline in numbers working in that region of the UK. O'Hara and Thomas (2014) is good for an account of how the range of actions carried out by the state that came to be known as austerity has affected the context of life in Britain. This includes the way that the government set about reducing the size of the public sector and which included making many thousands of workers redundant. Charlesworth (2000) provides a similar account to that of Jones, of another once-industrial town, Rotherham, and demonstrates the changes that have been brought about by the decline of industry in the UK. This is usually referred to as deindustrialisation. In one sense we can accept that work does change, that industries do decline for many reasons. However, in the UK this did not just happen, the state had a part to play in this change.

Deindustrialisation refers to the decline of industry within a country's economy and the move towards a focus on services, (Greenstein, 2019). One thing that Greenstein notes is that this change is often associated with a move towards service sector jobs and with lower wages. Industrial workers have often earned higher wages than service sector workers. Deindustrialisation within the UK has taken place over a long time (Nettleingham, 2019) but the mining industry declined very quickly and led to real social problems as a consequence of large numbers of men in particular becoming unemployed, often in areas where alternative employment was scarce (Strangleman, 2018).

This seems to be moving away from a concern with children and families. However, one thing that you should always ask as a student is 'so what'. This is a good time to ask that question. So what, why is this relevant to children, families and the state? It is relevant because we could say that deindustrialisation was a government strategy. The Conservative Government of the 1980s, led by Margaret Thatcher acted in ways which actively contributed to deindustrialisation. The families in Jones' study then can be seen to be much poorer as a consequence of deindustrialisation in general, and the decline of the mining industry in particular, than they had been before.

We can also say then that if we are looking at the lives of these families, and the children who live in them, it has been shaped to some extent by the actions that were taken by the state. So now we have a number of examples of the ways in which the state has an impact upon the lives of children and families; consider three in particular. Firstly in respect of services that are provided to support them such as welfare support or service provision such as Sure Start Children's Centres. Secondly, by pursuing economic and industrial strategies which can advantage or disadvantage families, and thirdly, in the way that the state has shaped the nature of housing.

So, we can see how the state has the power to change the context in which we live our lives. As an example of how the state can shape the environmental conditions under which we live it is useful to consider inequality in a more general way as it is starting to appear that many of the problems that are faced by families within the UK have a link to inequality.

3.4   Inequality

If we think about chapter 2 and the earlier sections of chapter 3 what stands out is that social inequality plays a large part in the problems that families experience. That may be terms of not having sufficient work in troubled families or it may be in terms of the instability that is built-in to the private rented sector of housing.

For example, what stands out in relation to troubled families is the extent to which these are poor families. This contributes to the overlap between troubled families and the underclass thesis. In terms of the underclass thesis, one thing that Mann (1992) argues is that when the economy is doing less well and more people find themselves without work the idea of an underclass, albeit sometimes given a different name, becomes a social concern. However, when the economy picks up then we find that the underclass disappears as the unemployed find work.

However, Mann was writing at the end of the 1980s. Things are different now. What stands out in the early 2020s is that those individuals and families who can be said to be poor now are often in work. From 2011/12 the majority of people in poverty were in working families, (Hick and Lanau, 2018, McBride et al., 2018, MacInnes et al., 2013). In 2018, 1 in 8 workers were classified as being poor, (Robb, 2018). This is partly as a consequence of a fall in the number of semi-skilled jobs alongside a rise in unskilled jobs but also because of low wages and a national minimum wage which is not sufficiently high enough. The UK Poverty Report 2018 from the Joseph Rowntree Foundation (2018) notes that:

- In our society there are now almost four million workers in poverty, a rise of over half a million compared with five years ago and the highest number on record.

- The employment rate is also at a record high, but this has not delivered lower poverty.

- Since 2004/05, the number of workers in poverty has increased at a faster rate than the total number of people in employment, resulting in workers being increasingly likely to find themselves in poverty.

The issue of in-work poverty is important as is the role that the state may have in addressing it in terms of strategies to alleviate poverty. For example, the National Minimum Wage has not always existed. The National Minimum Wage was introduced on 1 April 1999 by Tony Blair's Labour Government. Proposals to introduce a minimum wage were resisted just as proposals that men and women should receive equal pay were also resisted in the 1970s.

The National Minimum Wage should be seen alongside the Blair Governments aim to get more people in to work alongside their claims that work is the route out of poverty. 20 years after the introduction of a minimum wage, and in response to a claim by the Resolution Foundation predicting that child poverty will increase to its highest level for 60yrs a Conservative Government spokesperson noted that "we are committed to tackling child poverty and have made progress ... with 730,000 fewer children in workless households." (Mason et al., 2019). The problem should be obvious: if work is no longer a route out of poverty then getting more parents into work will not be the solution to child poverty unless something changes with respect to wages.

For families with 3 or more children, child poverty fell from 2007-08 but since then it has risen faster than for families with fewer children and is almost back to the level it was in 1996-7, (48%) just before the Labour Government under Blair came to power. As a student your task might be how are we able to explain this? We could point to the two-child limit on benefits and tax credits but this only came into effect in April 2017 so it has to be something else. Think instead about what has happened to wages in recent decades.

It is worth considering pay across time. It is easy to find details about pay using data from the Office for National Statistics (ONS). Visit www.ons.gov.uk. We always have to be careful when we look at data. For example the ONS illustrates that average weekly pay in January 2000 was £293.39. By December 2019 that had risen to £511.61. So, over 20 years average weekly pay had risen by £218.22. But as a student you always have to ask 'So what?' we know that prices go up over time, this is what we call inflation, so what is this increase worth?

Fortunately the ONS provide not only the figure for average weekly wages as they were in any given month since 2000, they illustrate what this really means, what they call real wages. As such the ONS reports that for average wages: "The figure in real terms (constant 2015 prices) is £474 per week, which is £1 (0.1%) higher than the pre-economic downturn peak of £473 per week for March 2008." (ONS, 2020). So, the value of wages now is £1 more than it was in March 2008.

A further problem for poorer workers is in what can be called under-employment. This refers to a situation where a worker would work longer hours if possible, for example, workers who are employed on part-time contracts but who want full-time contracts. Alongside this though, and maybe more importantly, is the growth in precarious and insecure work. This has come to be referred to as the gig economy, (Choonara, 2019, MacDonald and Giazitzoglu, 2019, Gross et al., 2018, Gerrard, 2017).

Work in the gig economy reflects the zero hours contracts that increasing numbers of workers find themselves on. This work is insecure because it is not stable. Remember that we said that stability is important for children so consider what it means for a child in a family where wages are not stable. Workers on zero hours contracts cannot be certain that they will have the same amount of work each week so they cannot trust that their income will be the same. This makes forward planning difficult.

Similar problems are experienced by workers who are compelled to be self-employed as this will mean that workers are denied benefits such as employment related sick pay or pensions. You could watch the film "Sorry we missed you" by director, Ken Loach to get an understanding of what this means for families (and justifiably say that you are studying!). For many insecure workers the welfare system provides some support however the value of welfare benefits in the UK have fallen as a consequence of policy changes introduced under the umbrella term austerity. The growth of poverty within the UK, can be evidenced in the growing number of children whose parents rely on foodbanks, (O'Hara, 2020, Lambie-Mumford and Green, 2017).

It is also worth considering inequalities relating to wealth. There is an argument which suggests that inequalities, especially pay inequalities, have social benefits in that it motivates us to work harder. This raises a question though in that although many people would readily accept that some jobs should be paid more than others, what is an acceptable difference? This is relevant because of the way in which inequalities in pay have become much wider since the early 1980s. Wilkinson and Pickett (2018, 2010) have researched the impact that inequality has on society extensively. Their argument is that inequalities have a negative effect on society irrespective of how wealthy any country is. This is relevant to children and families because although the UK is very wealthy compared to other countries it is also very unequal especially when compared to similar countries.

What is also important is that inequalities are getting wider, (Lyndon, 2019). The problem within the UK is not that we are a poor country; the problem is with how wealth is distributed. If you have an assignment relating to inequalities you will find it very useful to have a look at the Equality trust website online at https://www.equalitytrust.org.uk/. It will provide you with a lot of information about inequality in the UK. Similarly, the Joseph Rowntree Foundation website, www.jrf.org.uk/ provides access to up-to-date information on inequalities in a range of issues.

What is evident then is that many children and families experience hardships as a consequence of social inequalities. This is illustrated in a report by the United Nations. During November 2018 the United Nations sent a Special Rapporteur, Philip Alston, to the UK with the task of investigating and reporting on poverty, (O'Hara, 2020). This is relevant to understanding life-chances. Alston notes that:

> "Although the United Kingdom is the world's fifth largest economy, one fifth of its population (14 million people) live in poverty, and 1.5 million of them experienced destitution in 2017. Policies of austerity introduced in 2010 continue largely unabated, despite the tragic social consequences. Close to 40 per cent of children are predicted to be living in poverty by 2021. Food banks have proliferated; homelessness and rough sleeping have increased greatly; tens of thousands of poor families must live in accommodation far from their schools, jobs and community networks; life expectancy is falling for certain groups; and the legal aid system has been decimated. The social safety net has been badly damaged by drastic cuts to local authorities' budgets, which have eliminated many social services, reduced policing services, closed libraries in record numbers, shrunk community and youth centres and sold off public spaces and buildings. The bottom line is that much of the glue that has held British society together since the Second World War has been deliberately removed and replaced with a harsh and uncaring ethos. A booming economy, high employment and a budget surplus have not reversed austerity, a policy pursued more as an ideological than an economic agenda." (Alston, 2019)

I indicated above that the changes that have taken place within the UK are rarely by accident and that in general they are the consequences of political decisions and choices. Political ideologies will be explored more fully in Creasy (2020) Family, State and Policy but at this stage it is useful to reiterate that neoliberal ideology in particular underpins what came to be referred to as austerity. At the same time neoliberal policies since 1979 have weakened the position of workers in ways which have seen wages stagnating or falling. This is at the same time that the value of benefits have been reduced and access to them cut though this is also in line with neoliberal ideas. In considering what this might mean for poorer children and families in particular the UN report goes on to state that,

> "After years of progress, child poverty has been rising since 2011–2012, almost entirely in working families. The Equality and Human Rights Commission forecasts that 1.5 million more children will fall into poverty between 2010 and 2021–2022, bringing the child poverty rate to a shocking 41 per cent. One in 10 girls in the United Kingdom has been unable to afford menstrual products, and many have missed school because of their period. Changes to benefits, and sanctions against parents, have unintended consequences on children and are driving the increase in child poverty. The Child Poverty Action Group found that Child Benefit will have lost 23 per cent of its real value between 2010 and 2020, due to sub-inflationary uprating and the current freeze. And low-paid jobs and stagnant wages have a direct effect on children, with families where two adults earn the minimum wage still falling 11 per cent short of the adequate income needed to raise a child." (p16)

With this in mind it is apparent that a child's family shapes their lived experiences as a child and also influences their future. It is always important however to distinguish between the problems that a family experiences and the factors which contribute to it. Ridge (2013) is useful in terms of understanding what poverty means for children. Similarly, Rose and McAuley (2019) provide evidence from parents experiencing poverty in terms of their experiences and O'Hara (2020) draws upon lots of accounts of experiencing poverty including the authors own experiences.

3.5 Using chapter 3

So, at this point we have to think about how to use this chapter and in some ways this chapter has been a little less obvious in terms of structure. A little less focused perhaps in what it covers because it covered things which seem quite distinct. We could ask why it was that I started with a section on housing and that would be a fair question. So, as I try to explain myself I want you to think that you have to do the same when you write assignments.

I started with housing because chapter 2 ended with the idea of failing families as an underclass and when I read about the underclass, or about failing families I often think about housing and what happens within the home. I see pictures of housing in disrepair and housing that is generally untidy or which appears uncared for. I then think about what it means for children who live in these areas. I also think about the ways in which we can provide housing and in recent years I can't help but think that the state has done things which have created some problems such as promoting the growth of renting from private landlords. It is evident that this has pushed housing costs up and lowered standards at the same time.

So, for me, it seemed that starting with housing and then moving on to social mobility would work. You will see later though that if you have an assignment on poverty or inequality you might use this chapter very differently. That is fine. But if you were to write an assignment which considered housing I think there are some key points that I would expect to be included:

- The home is central to family life and is generally seen as being a source of stability in children's lives;
- The landscape of housing is shaped by the state;
- The last 30 years have seen a significant growth in

the Private Rented Sector and this often provides poor quality housing in a way which reduces stability because it is insecure;
- Changes to the welfare system such as the 'Bedroom Tax' have made life harder for families who rely on welfare benefits and there has been a move towards making the welfare system harsh.

So, although housing is important in terms of how it establishes the base for children's lives one thing that chapter 3 has demonstrated is that it is possible to escape poverty, that children are not destined to experience poverty just because their parents did. We refer to this as being upwardly socially mobile. If you are writing about social mobility then there are some key issues that were covered in this section:

- Social mobility is a consequence of social and economic conditions more than a consequence of ability or merit;
- Social mobility is not a solution to poverty at a social level, only at a personal level;
- Life-chances is the term that is used when referring to a person's potential future.

Within this chapter I set out an argument which was structured in a way that considered the nature of housing in the UK and which focused on the insecurity and instability which often results from renting from a private landlord. In doing this I was establishing that for some children, their home contributes to some of the disadvantages that they may face. This followed on from previous discussions about families experiencing poverty. I then went on to say that although some children may experience disadvantage we must be careful not to see this in a deterministic way. Children can escape poverty and disadvantage. The discussion of social mobility provided material which explored that.

As such the final section used Bronfenbrenner's socio-ecological model to frame a broader understanding of a child's environment. Personally I struggled in terms of deciding where to do this. I chose to do it at the end to show how you might make sense of poverty, housing and social mobility but it would make just as much sense to have section 3.3 as 3.1. There are no hard and fast rules. You have to think about how you will structure your argument.

So, if we wanted to construct an assignment which demonstrated why it is necessary to consider the role of the state when studying children and families we could start by referring to Bronfenbrenner's ecological model and note that when it comes to the:

- Microsystem, the state has influence over aspects such as schools and Early Years provision;

- Exosystem, the state has influence over social services, the economy and the nature of parents work experiences;

- Macrosystem, the state can influence social and cultural attitudes and values.

We could then offer a bit more detail by turning to some of the descriptions of families in Jones (2016) to point to ways in which the government of the 1980s acted in ways which had significant consequences for many industrial workers. You might find it necessary to explain deindustrialisation in doing this. You might develop an argument which does more to say "so what". For example, Jones (2016) illustrates how changes over which the family has no control over exert a significant pressure upon the shape of the family. The main point here is that many families have struggled under the impact of deindustrialisation but what he then points out is that when it comes to unwanted social behaviours or social patterns the family is seen to be at fault.

So, the key points from section 3.3 for me are that:
- Bronfenbrenner provides an understanding of child de-

velopment which brings the social environment to the fore;
- The different systems (the rings) in Bronfenbrenner's socio-ecological model illustrate the part played by the family, the community, the state, and the way in which social structures and organisations have an impact on the child's lived experience;
- What happens within each of the systems is not fixed, it changes over time;
- Bronfenbrenner's model underpinned the development of social policies such as Sure Start in the UK;

To complete the chapter, to join the circle so to speak, I ended with a section on inequality. This drew on some issues covered in earlier chapters also in that many of the problems experienced by children and families are problems which have their roots within inequality. The UK is a very unequal country compared to other european countries and this inevitably impacts upon children and families. So, an essay on inequality could use the material from section 3.4, to establish evidence of inequality and then go to section 3.1 on housing as a particular example. You could then use section 3.3, Bronfenbrenner as a way into to considering how the state may address inequality and use the examples of Headstart and Sure Start. I adopted one approach but you have to use the evidence from your reading to suit what you want to say. One thing that you really can't avoid, and really shouldn't scrimp on as a student is reading. Read as much as you can.

In saying this though we are moving away from the school experiences that you may have had within which there is a correct answer to all assignment questions. In that system all you have to do is learn the correct answer, which you might see as content, or what goes in an assignment, and then reproduce the correct answer in an essay or exam. Studying in Higher Education is not the same. Very often you have to focus much more on what you do with content. Higher marks do not come from having the right content. Higher marks come from using it more effectively; by being logical and structured and by writing in clear and concise ways.

REFERENCES

ALLEN 2011. Early Intervention: The Next steps. London: Cabinet Office.

ALMOND, B. 2008. *The Fragmenting Family*, OUP Oxford.

ALSTON, P. 2019. Visit to the United Kingdom of Great Britain and Northern Ireland: Report of the Special Rapporteur on extreme poverty and human rights. United Nations.

ANDREWS, J., HUTCHINSON, J. & JOHNES, R. 2016. Grammar Schools and Social Mobility. London: Education Policy Instutute.

ANNING, A. & BALL, M. 2008. *Improving services for young children: from Sure Start to children's centres,* London, SAGE.

BAGGULEY, P. & MANN, K. 1992. Idle Thieving Bastards? Scholarly Representations of the `Underclass'. *Work, Employment and Society,* 6, 113-126.

BAILEY, N. 2020. Poverty and the re-growth of private renting in the UK, 1994-2018. *PLoS ONE*, Vol 15, Issue 2, pp263-74.

BALL, E., BATTY, E. & FLINT, J. 2016. Intensive Family Intervention and the Problem Figuration of 'Troubled Families'. *Social Policy & Society,* 15, 2, 263-74.

BAUMAN, Z. 2000. *Liquid modernity,* Cambridge, Polity Press.

BAUMAN, Z. 2003. *Liquid love: on the frailty of human bonds,* Cambridge, Polity.

BECK, U. & BECK-GERNSHEIM, E. 1995. *The Normal Chaos of Love,* Cambridge, Polity.

BOM, I., VAN DER, PATERSON, L. L., PEPLOW, D. & GRAINGER, K. 2018. 'It's not the fact they claim benefits but their useless, lazy, drug taking lifestyles we despise': Analysing audience responses to Benefits Street using live tweets. *Discourse, Context & Media,* 21,1, 36-45.

BONE, J. 2014. Neoliberal Nomads: Housing Insecurity and the Revival of Private Renting in the UK.

BOSELY, S. 2020. Austerity blamed for life expectancy stalling for first time in century. *The Guardian*.

BRONFENBRENNER, U. 1979. *The ecology of human development: Experiments by nature and design,* Cambridge, MA, Harvard University Press.

CAIN, R. 2016. Responsibilising recovery: lone and low-paid parents, Universal

Credit and the gendered contradictions of UK welfare reform. *British Politics*, Vol. 11 Issue 4, p488-507.

CALDER, G. 2016. How inequality runs in families : Unfair advantage and the limits of social mobility. Bristol: Policy Press.

CALDER, G. 2018. What Would a Society Look Like Where Children's Life Chances Were Really Fair? *Local Economy*, 33, 6, 655-666.

CASEY, L. C. B. 2014. The National Troubled Families Programme. *Social Work & Social Sciences Review*, 17, 57-62.

CHAMBERS, D. 2001. *Representing the family*, London, SAGE.

CHARLESWORTH, S. J. 2000. *A phenomenology of working class experience*, Cambridge, Cambridge Univ. Press.

CHILD, P. 2018. Landlordism, Rent Regulation and the Labour Party in mid-twentieth century Britain, 1950-64. *Twentieth Century British History*, Vol. 29 Issue 1, p79-103.

CHOONARA, J. 2019. *Insecurity, Precarious Work and Labour Markets: Challenging the Orthodoxy*, Cham, Springer International Publishing.

COE, R., JONES, K., SEARLE, J., KOKOTSAKI, D., MOHD KOSNIN, A. & SKINNER, P. 2008. Evidence on the effects of selective educational systems. Durham: CEM Centre, Durham University.

CORBY, F., H. 2015. Parenting Support: How Failing Parents Understand the Experience. *Journal of Education & Social Policy*, 2, 2, 38-46.

COULTER, R. 2017. Social Disparities in Private Renting Amongst Young Families in England and Wales, 2001-2011. *Housing, Theory & Society*, 34, 3, 297-322.

CPAG. 2019. *CHILD POVERTY IN WORKING FAMILIES ON THE RISE* [Online]. London: Child Poverty Action Group. Available: https://cpag.org.uk/news-blogs/news-listings/child-poverty-working-families-rise [Accessed 20/03/2020 2020].

CREASY, R. 2018. *The Taming of Education*, Basingstoke, Palgrave.

CREASY, R. 2020a. *Family, State & Policy: A critical introduction for Childhood Studies*, York, Independent.

CREASY, R. 2020b. *Resilience, Risk & Safeguarding: A critical introduction for childhood studies*, York, Independent.

CREASY, R. 2020c. *Wellbeing, Vulnerability & Life-chances: A critical introduction for Childhood Studies*, York, Independent.

CREASY, R. & CORBY, F. 2019. *Taming childhood?: a critical perspective on policy, practice and parenting*, Basingstoke, Hampshire, Palgrave Macmillan.

CROSSLEY, S. 2015. The Troubled Families Programme: the perfect social policy? *In: CCJS Briefing paper.* London: Centre for crime and justice studies.

CROSSLEY, S. 2018a. *Troublemakers: The construction of 'troubled families' as a social problem,* Bristol, Bristol University Press.

CROSSLEY, S. 2018b. The UK Government's Troubled Families Programme: Delivering Social Justice? *Social Inclusion*, Vo 6, issue 1, 301-9.

DAVIES, A. 2013. 'Right to Buy': The Development of a Conservative Housing Policy, 1945–1980. *Contemporary British History,* Vol. 27 Issue 4, p421-444.

DEAN, H. 1991. Patterns and experiences of unemployment. *In:* BROWN, P. & SCASE, R. (eds.) *Poor work: disadvantage and the division of labour,* Milton Keynes: Open University Press.

DICKERSON, A. & POPLI, G. 2018. The Many Dimensions of Child Poverty: Evidence from the UK Millennium Cohort Study*. *Fiscal Studies,* Vol. 39 Issue 2, p265-298.

DISNEY, R. & LUO, G. 2017. The Right to Buy public housing in Britain: A welfare analysis. *Journal of Housing Economics,* 35, 51-68.

DONETTO, S. & MABEN, J. 2015. 'These places are like a godsend': a qualitative analysis of parents' experiences of health visiting outside the home and of children's centres services. *Health Expectations, Vol18, issue 6, pp2559-70.*

DRIVER, S. & MARTELL, L. 1998. *New Labour: Politics after Thatcherism,* Cambridge, Polity Press.

FATTORE, T., MASON, J. & WATSON, E. 2007. Children's Conceptualisation(s) of Their Well-Being. *Social Indicators Research.* Vol 80, Issue 1, pp5-29

FERGUSON, H. 2003. Welfare, social exclusion and reflexivity: the case of child and woman protection. *Journal of Social Policy*, Vol. 32 Issue 2, pp199-217.

FIELD, F. 2010. The Foundation Years: preventing poor children becoming poor adults,. London: Cabinet Office.

FLETCHER, A., GARDNER, F., MCKEE, M. & BONELL, C. 2012. The British government's Troubled Families Programme: A flawed response to riots and youth offending. *BMJ: British Medical Journal,* 344, 7860, p8.

FLETCHER, D. R. & WRIGHT, S. 2018. A hand up or a slap down? Criminalising benefit claimants in Britain via strategies of surveillance, sanctions and deterrence. *Critical Social Policy,* Vol. 38 Issue 2, p323-344.

FROST, N. 2011. *Rethinking children and families: the relationship between childhood, families and the state,* London: Continuum International Publishing

Group.

GARRETT, P. B. 2018. *Welfare words: critical social work & social policy,* London, Sage.

GARRETT, P. M. 2007. 'Sinbin' solutions: The 'pioneer' projects for 'problem families' and the forgetfulness of social policy research. *Critical Social Policy,* 27, 2, 203-230.

GERRARD, J. 2017. *Precarious Enterprise on the Margins: Work, Poverty, and Homelessness in the City,* New York, Palgrave Macmillan US.

GILBERT, A. 2018. *British conservatism and the legal regulation of intimate relationships,* Oxford, Hart Publishing.

GILLIES, V., HORSLEY, N. & EDWARDS, R. 2017. *Challenging the politics of early intervention: who's 'saving' children and why,* Bristol, Policy Press.

GOLDTHORPE, J., H. 2016a. Decades of investment in education have not improved social mobility. *The Guardian.*

GOLDTHORPE, J., H 2016b. Social class mobility in modern Britain: changing structure, constant process. *Journal of the British Academy,* 4, 2, pp89-111.

GREENSTEIN, J. 2019. Development Without Industrialization? Household Well-Being and Premature Deindustrialization. *Journal of Economic Issues,* 53, 3, 612-633.

GREGG, D. 2010. Family intervention projects: a classic case of policy-based evidence. *Evidence-based policy.* London: Centre for Crime and Justice Studies.

GROSS, S.-A., MUSGRAVE, G. & JANCIUTE, L. 2018. *Well-being and mental health in the gig economy: policy perspectives on precarity,* London, University of Westminster Press.

GUARDIAN, T. 2002. *Full text of Tony Blair's speech on welfare reform* [Online]. London: Guardian News and Media.

HALL, J., EISENSTADT, N., SYLVA, K., SMITH, T., SAMMONS, P., SMITH, G., EVANGELOU, M., GOFF, J., TANNER, E., AGUR, M. & HUSSEY, D. 2015. A Review of the Services Offered by English Sure Start Children's Centres in 2011 and 2012. *Oxford Review of Education.Vol 41, issue 1, pp89-105*

HASKEY, J., KIERNAN, K., DAVID, M. E. & MORGAN, P. M. 1998. *The fragmenting family: does it matter?,* IEA Health and Welfare Unit.

HICK, R. O. D. & LANAU, A. 2018. Moving In and Out of In-work Poverty in the UK: An Analysis of Transitions, Trajectories and Trigger Events. *Journal of Social Policy,* Vol. 47 Issue 4, p661-682.

HIRSCH, D. 2018. The 'living wage' and low income: Can adequate pay contribute to adequate family living standards? *Critical Social Policy,* 38, 2, 367-386.

HM GOVERNMENT 2020. *Government confirms extra support for Troubled Families to succeed.* London: Ministry of Housing, Communities, and Local Government

HOGGETT, J. & FROST, E. 2018. The Troubled Families Programme and the Problems of Success. *Social Policy & Society,* Vol. 17 Issue 4, p523-534.

HOGHUGHI, M. & LONG, N. 2004. *Handbook of parenting: theory and research for practice,* London, SAGE.

HOLT, A. 2010. Managing `Spoiled Identities': Parents' Experiences of Compulsory Parenting Support Programmes. Great Britain: John Wiley & Sons, Ltd.

HUGHES, M., WIKELY, F. & NASH, T. 1994. *Parents and their Children's Schools,* Oxford, Blackwell.

INGLIS, D. & THORPE, C. 2019. *An invitation to social theory,* Cambridge, Polity.

JAMES, A. & PROUT, A. 1997. *Constructing and reconstructing childhood: contemporary issues in the sociological study of childhood,* London, Falmer.

JENSEN, T. 2018. The cultural industry of parent-blame. *Parenting the crisis.* 1 ed.: Bristol University Press.

JONES, G. 2007. Assessing the Success of the Sale of Social Housing in the UK. *Journal of Social Welfare & Family Law,* 29, 2, 135-150.

JONES, O. 2012. *Chavs: the demonization of the working class,* London, Verso.

JONES, O. 2016. *Chavs: the demonization of the working class,* London, Verso.

JONES, P. & BRADBURY, L. 2018. *Introducing social theory,* Cambridge, Polity Press.

JORDAN, B. 1973. *Paupers: The Making of the New Claiming Class,* London, Routledge and Kegan Paul.

JRF. 2018. *UK Poverty 2018* [Online]. York: Joseph Rowntree Foundation. Available: https://www.jrf.org.uk/report/uk-poverty-2018 [Accessed 20 March 2020].

JUPP, E. 2017. Families, policy and place in times of austerity. *Area. 49, 3, 266-73*

KEMP, P. A. 2015. Private Renting After the Global Financial Crisis. *Housing Studies,* 30, 4, 601-620.

KING, P. 2010. *Housing policy transformed: the right to buy and the desire to own,* Bristol: Policy Press.

KNOWLES, G. & HOLMSTROM, R. 2013. *Understanding family diversity and home-school relations: a guide for students and practitioners in early years and primary settings,* London, Routledge.

LAMBERT, M. 2019. Between 'Families in Trouble' and 'Children at Risk': Historicising 'Troubled Family' Policy in England since 1945. *Children & Society,* Vol. 33 Issue 1, p82-92

LAMBIE-MUMFORD, H. & GREEN, M. A. 2017. Austerity, welfare reform and the rising use of food banks by children in England and Wales. *Area.* 49, 3, 273-279

LAREAU, A. 2011. *Unequal childhoods: class, race, and family life,* London, University of California Press.

LEVITAS, R. 1998. *The inclusive society?: social exclusion and new labour,* Basingstoke, Palgrave.

LEVITAS, R. 2012. There may be 'trouble' ahead: what we know about those 120,000 'troubled' families *Poverty Response Series.* Poverty and Social Exclusion in the UK https://www.poverty.ac.uk/system/files/WP%20Policy%20Response%20No.3-%20%20'Trouble'%20ahead%20(Levitas%20Final%2021April2012).pdf

LEWIS, J. 2011. Parenting programmes in England: policy development and implementation issues, 2005-2010. *Journal of Social Welfare & Family Law.* 33, 2, 107-122

LEWIS, J., CUTHBERT, R. & SARRE, S. 2011. What are Children's Centres? The Development of CC Services, 2004-2008. *Social Policy & Administration.* 45, 1, 35-54

LINDSAY, G., STRAND, S. & DAVIS, H. 2011. A comparison of the effectiveness of three parenting programmes in improving parenting skills, parent mental-well being and children's behaviour when implemented on a large scale in community settings in 18 English local authorities: the parenting early intervention pathfinder (PEIP). *BMC Public Health,* Vol 11, Issue 1, p 962.

LINDSAY, G., TOTSIKA, V. & THOMAS, R. 2019. Evaluating Parent Gym: a community implemented universal parenting programme. *Journal of Children's Services,* Vol. 14 Issue 1, p1-15.

LUND, B. 2016. *Housing Politics in the United Kingdom: power, planning and protest,* Bristol, Policy Press.

LYNDON, S. 2019. Troubling Discourses of Poverty in Early Childhood in the UK. *Children & Society,* 33, 6, 602-609.

MACDONALD, R. & GIAZITZOGLU, A. 2019. Youth, enterprise and precarity: or, what is, and what is wrong with, the 'gig economy'? *Journal of Sociology,* 55, 4, 724-740.

MACDONALD, R., SHILDRICK, T. & FURLONG, A. 2014. In search of 'intergenerational cultures of worklessness': Hunting the Yeti and shooting zombies. Critical Social policy, 34 2, p199-p220

MACINNES, T., ALDRIDGE, H., BUSHE, S., KENWAY, P. & TINSON, A. 2013. MONITORING POVERTY AND SOCIAL EXCLUSION 2013. York: Joseph Rowntree Foundation.

MANN, K. 1992. *The Making of an English 'Underclass'? The Social Divisions of Welfare and Labour,* Milton Keynes, Open University Press.

MARMOT, M. 2015. 'The richer you are, the better your health – and how this can be changed'. *The Guardian,* 11 September 2015.

MASON, R., PROCTOR, K. & ELLIOTT, L. 2019. Fears child poverty may rise to record 60-year high under Tories. *The Guardian.*

MCBRIDE, J., SMITH, A. & MBALA, M. 2018. 'You End Up with Nothing': The Experience of Being a Statistic of 'In-Work Poverty' in the UK. *Work, Employment & Society,* 32, 210-218.

MCCULLOCH, D. 2017. Austerity's Impact on Rough Sleeping and Violence. *In:* COOPER, V. & WHYTE, D. (eds.) *The Violence of Austerity.* Pluto Press.

MENDE, M., SCOTT, M. L., GARVEY, A. M. & BOLTON, L. E. 2019. The marketing of love: how attachment styles affect romantic consumption journeys. *Journal of the Academy of Marketing Science,* 47, 2, 255-273.

MORGAN, D. H. J. 2011. *Rethinking Family Practices,* Basingstoke, Palgrave Macmillan.

MORGAN, D. H. J., MCCARTHY, J. R., GILLIES, V. & HOOPER, C.-A. 2019. Family Troubles, Troubling Families, and Family Practices. *Journal of Family Issues,* 40, 16, 2225-2238.

MOSS, P., DILLON, J. & STATHAM, J. 2000. The 'child in need' and 'the rich child': discourses, constructions and practice. *Critical Social Policy,* 20, 2, 233-255.

MULLIN, A. 2012. The Ethical and Social Significance of Parenting: A Philosophical Approach. *Parenting: Science & Practice,* 12, 2/3, 134-143.

MUNRO, L. 2019. Life Chances, Education and Social Movements. London, UK; New York, NY, USA: Anthem Press.

MURIE, A. 2016. *The right to buy?: selling off public and social housing,* Bristol, UK, Policy Press.

MURRAY, C. 1984. *Losing ground: American social policy, 1950-1980,* BasicBooks.

MURRAY, C., LISTER, R., HEALTH, I. O. E. A. & UNIT, W. 1996. Charles Murray and the underclass: the developing debate. London: bInstitute of Economic Affairs, Health and Welfare Unit.

NECKERMAN, K. M. 1993. The Emergence of "Underclass" Family Patterns, 1900-1940. *In:* KATZ, M. B. (ed.) *The "Underclass" Debate.* Princeton University Press.

NETTLEINGHAM, D. 2019. Beyond the heartlands: deindustrialization, naturalization and the meaning of an 'industrial' tradition. *British Journal of Sociology,* 70, 2, 610-626.

NICOLSON, P. 2014. *A critical approach to human growth and development,* Basingstoke, Palgrave Macmillan.

NIXON, J. 2007. Deconstructing 'problem' researchers and 'problem' families: a rejoinder to Garrett. *Critical Social Policy,* 27, 4, 546-556.

O'HARA, M. 2020. *The Shame Game: Overturning the Toxic Narrative of Poverty,* Bristol, Policy Press.

O'HARA, M. & THOMAS, M. 2014. *Austerity bites: a journey to the sharp end of cuts in th UK,* Bristol, Policy Press.

ONS. 2020. *Average weekly earnings in Great Britain: February 2020* [Online]. London: Office for National Statistics. Available: https://www.ons.gov.uk/employmentandlabourmarket/peopleinwork/employmentandemployeetypes/bulletins/averageweeklyearningsingreatbritain/february2020 [Accessed 20 March 2020].

PAGE, R. M. 2015. *Clear blue water?: the Conservative Party and the welfare state since 1940,* Bristol, Policy Press.

PARR, S. 2017. Explaining and Understanding State Intervention into the Lives of 'Troubled' Families. *Social Policy & Society,* 16, 4, 577.

PARTON, N. 2006. *Safeguarding childhood: early intervention and surveillance in a late modern society,* Basingstoke,, Palgrave Macmillan.

PATERSON, L., L., COFFEY-GLOVER, L. & PEPLOW, D. 2016. Negotiating stance within discourses of class: Reactions to Benefits Street. *Discourse & Society,* 27, 2, 195.

PINTO, S. 2017. Researching romantic love. *Rethinking History,* 21, 4, 567-585.

REAY, D. 2017. *Miseducation: inequality, education and the working classes,* Bristol, Policy Press.

RIDGE, T. 2013. 'We are All in This Together'? The Hidden Costs of Poverty, Recession and Austerity Policies on Britain's Poorest Children. *Children &*

Society, 27, 5, 406-417.

ROBB, C. 2018. *More people in work, but many still trapped in poverty.* York: Joseph Rowntree trust

ROSE, W. & MCAULEY, C. 2019. Poverty and its impact on parenting in the UK: Re-defining the critical nature of the relationship through examining lived experiences in times of austerity. *Children and Youth Services Review,* 97, 134-141.

ROYSTON, S. 2017. Welfare reform and the 'family test'. *Broken benefits.* 1 ed.: Bristol University Press.

RUNCIMAN, W. G. 1990. How many Classes are there in Contemporary British Society? *Sociology,* 24, 3, 377-396.

SALTIEL, D. 2013. Understanding complexity in families' lives: the usefulness of -family practices- as an aid to decision-making. Great Britain: Blackwell Publishing Ltd.

SCHWEIGER, G. & GRAF, G. 2015. *A philosophical examination of social justice and child poverty,* Basingstoke, Palgrave Macmillan.

SHAW, B., WATSON, B., FRAUENDIENST, B., REDECKER, A., JONES, T. & HILLMAN, M. 2013. Children's independent mobility: a comparative study in England and Germany (1971-2010). London: Policy Studies Institute

SIMPSON, D., LUMSDEN, E. & MCDOWALL CLARK, R. 2015. Neoliberalism, global poverty policy and early childhood education and care: a critique of local uptake in England. *Early Years,* 35, 1, 96-109.

SIRAJ-BLATCHFORD, I., MAYO, A., MELHUISH, E., TAGGART, B., SAMMONS, P. & SYLVA, K. 2013. The learning life course of at 'risk' children aged 3-16: Perceptions of students and parents about 'succeeding against the odds'. *Scottish Educational Review,* 42, 2, 5-17.

SIRAJ, I. & MAYO, A. 2014. *Social class and educational inequality: the impact of parents and schools,* Cambridge, Cambridge University Press.

SMART, C. 2007. *Personal Life,* Oxford, Wiley.

SMITH, K. M. 2014. *The government of childhood: discourse, power and subjectivity,* Basingstoke, Palgrave Macmillan.

SMITH, M. J. 1998. *Social Science in Question* London, Sage.

STEEL, L., KIDD, W. & BROWN, A. 2012. *The family,* Basingstoke, Palgrave Macmillan.

STRANGLEMAN, T. 2018. 'Mining a productive seam? The coal industry, community and sociology'. *Contemporary British History,* Vol. 32 Issue 1, p18-38.

THATCHER, M. T. F. 1987. *Interview for Woman's Own ("no such thing as society")* [Online]. Available: https://www.margaretthatcher.org/document/106689 [Accessed 17 September 2019].

THOMPSON, N. 2017. *Social problems and social justice,* London, Palgrave.

TISDALL, L. 2017. Education, parenting and concepts of childhood in England, c. 1945 to c. 1979. *Contemporary British History,* 31, 1, 24-46.

VINCENT, C. & MAXWELL, C. 2016. Parenting priorities and pressures: furthering understanding of 'concerted cultivation'. *Discourse: Studies in the Cultural Politics of Education.* 37, 2, 269-82

WALKER, S. 2020. 'Baby machines': eastern Europe's answer to depopulation. *The Guardian.*

WALKERDINE, V. 2009. developmental psychology and the study of childhood. *In:* KEHILY, M. J. (ed.) *An Introduction to Childhood.* second ed. Maidenhead: Open University press.

WELLS, K. 2018. *Childhood Studies,* Cambridge, Polity.

WELSHMAN, J. 1999. The Social History of Social Work: The Issue of the 'Problem Family', 1940-70. *British Journal of Social Work,* 29, 3, 457-476.

WELSHMAN, J. 2013. *Underclass: a history of the excluded since 1880,* London, Bloomsbury Academic.

WHALLEY, M. & CENTRE, P. G. 2007. *Involving parents in their children's learning,* London, Paul Chapman.

WHEELER, S. 'Essential assistance' versus 'concerted cultivation': theorising class-based patterns of parenting in Britain. 2018 Pedagogy, Culture & Society, 26, 3, 327-344.

WHITTAKER, K. A. & COWLEY, S. 2012. An Effective Programme Is Not Enough: A Review of Factors Associated with Poor Attendance and Engagement with Parenting Support Programmes. *Children & Society,* 26, 2, 138-149.

WILBY, P. 2020. The expert in social mobility who says education cannot make it happen. *The Guardian.*

WILDING, R. 2017. *Families, intimacy and globalization: floating ties,* Basingstoke, Hampshire, Palgrave Macmillan.

WILKINSON, R. G. & PICKETT, K. 2010. *The spirit level: why equality is better for everyone,* London, Penguin.

WILKINSON, R. G. & PICKETT, K. 2018. *The Inner Level: How More Equal Societies Reduce Stress, Restore Sanity and Improve Everyone's Wellbeing,* London, Allen Lane.

WRIGHT, S., FLETCHER, D. R. & STEWART, A. B. R. 2020. Punitive benefit sanctions, welfare conditionality, and the social abuse of unemployed people in Britain: Transforming claimants into offenders? *Social Policy & Administration,* Vol. 54 Issue 2, p278-294.

WYNESS, M. G. 2012. *Childhood and society,* Basingstoke, Palgrave Macmillan.

Finally

Many thanks for reading this, I hope that you found it useful and helpful. You are welcome to provide feedback and/or suggestions via my email address:
robcreasy@hotmail.co.uk

If you do want to get in touch you might provide a brief response to the following questions:

- Overall, was it useful? Is there anything that I should add or change?
- Have I got the tone right, is it too deep or not academic enough?
- Does it speak to you, does it make sense?

I do have a favour to ask though. I decided to self-publish this book because the prices that major publishers charge can be prohibitive. By self-publishing I can sell this, and other related books as referred to, for a small amount but that means that I don't have a marketing budget. So, two things will really help me:
1. Please recommend this book to friends;
2. Please leave a review on Amazon, having lots of good reviews in particular is really helpful.

Best wishes, Rob.

ABOUT THE AUTHOR

Dr Rob Creasy was previously Director of Social Sciences at York St John University in the UK. He has taught in Further Education and Higher Education for over 30 years. He is the author of "The Taming of Education" (2018) published by Palgrave Macmillan and the co-author of "Taming Childhood" (2019) also published by Palgrave Macmillan as well as a number of journal articles. He wasn't all that good at school and got his first "O" level aged 25. His undergraduate and postgraduate degrees are in Sociology, Social Policy and Education and he is a Senior Fellow of the Higher Education Academy. In 2015 he led the introduction of BA Sociology at York St John University; in 2019 this was ranked as the number 1 sociology course in the UK based on student satisfaction as reported in the National Student Satisfaction survey.

Printed in Great Britain
by Amazon